Jonathan Swift as a Tory Pamphleteer

Jonathan Swift in 1710

Jonathan Swift AS A TORY

PAMPHLETEER

BY RICHARD I. COOK

University of Washington Press
SEATTLE AND LONDON

Frontispiece from
the portrait of Swift in 1710 by
Charles Jervas in the National Portrait
Gallery. Reprinted by permission.

Preface

POLITICAL tracts, as such, are among the most perishable of literary commodities, and it is not surprising that, despite the renewed interest in Swift that the past fifty years have seen, the polemical works which he produced in behalf of the Tory campaign leading to the Peace of Utrecht have received relatively little attention from twentieth-century critics. Yet these tracts—for their intrinsic merit as examples of persuasive discourse, for the light they shed on Swift's use of rhetorical techniques during an important period in his development, and for the significant relationships they have with his more famous works—are worth closer study than they have hitherto received.

If one were to divide Swift's career into "periods," as has been so often done with other authors, the years 1710–14 would naturally fall into a "Middle Period." These were the years when, as all his biographers agree, Swift's career as a man of affairs was at its high-water mark. The nature and extent of Swift's influence in the Harley–St. John ministry have no doubt been frequently exaggerated, but it remains true that during these years Swift occupied a position which even in those days of author-politicians was impressive. While Swift may not have been the policy-maker some biographers have portrayed, he nevertheless functioned both as a close friend and an invaluable political instrument of the men who were guiding England's affairs, and it is natural that many of the fundamental attitudes toward politics and society which Swift developed during these years would color his later literary productions.

To consider Swift's political tracts as purely secondary and incidental to his more famous works is to overlook the facts that they are among the most accomplished examples of political writing in the English language and that they reflect some of Swift's deepest interests. Concerning the importance of Swift's political writings of the 1710–14 period, so eminent a Swift scholar as Ricardo Quintana has remarked: "*A Short Character of His Ex. The Earl of Wharton* and *The Conduct of the Allies,* to take two examples [of Swift's political journalism] . . . , are masterpieces in their way, more significant in respect of the author's art than many of his purely belletristic productions." [1] As Quintana indicates, the literary merit of Swift's Tory journalism (which in bulk alone forms more than a quarter of Swift's work in prose) is high, and the light such journalism sheds upon the great works which preceded and followed the political writings is considerable.

In the study of Swift's Tory tracts I have directed most of my attention toward discussion and analysis of specific rhetorical techniques and approaches in the tracts themselves. But in order to refresh the reader's memory of the biographical context in which these works appeared, I have thought it desirable to add an introduction which treats of such pertinent, though relatively familiar topics as Swift's early political history, his conversion to Toryism, and the nature and importance of his role in the Harley–St. John ministry. Likewise, with a view toward clarifying the significance of the Tory tracts in Swift's development as an artist, I have undertaken in Chapters One and Eight to survey—with special emphasis on intended audience and sense of political urgency—Swift's more important works written prior to 1710 and after 1714.

For invaluable advice and assistance, I am deeply indebted to Ernest Tuveson, Alain Renoir, Donald S. Taylor, Donald Cornu, and Bernard V. Burke. I would also like to thank the following journals for allowing me to reprint materials which have appeared, in somewhat altered form, in their pages: *The Huntington Library Quarterly* (June, 1961; February, 1966), *Texas Studies in Language and Literature* (Spring, 1962), *Studies in English Literature 1500–1900* (Summer, 1962), *Speech Monographs* (November, 1962), *Discourse* (Winter, 1963), and *The Modern Language Quarterly* (March, 1963).

1. Ricardo Quintana, *The Mind and Art of Jonathan Swift* (New York, 1953), p. 214.

Contents

Illustrations

Introduction: "A Person of Some Consequence"

I

ON September 20, 1710, two weeks after his arrival in London to petition the queen for royal funds toward the support of the Irish Church, Jonathan Swift wrote in his *Journal to Stella:*

We shall have a strange Winter here between the struggles of a cunning provoked discarded party, and the triumphs of one in power; of both which I shall be an indifferent spectator, and return very peaceably to Ireland, when I have done my part in the affair I am entrusted with, whether it succeeds or no.[1]

That Swift, despite his protestations, was a far from neutral bystander is indicated only a few lines earlier in the *Journal* where he remarks of the recently deposed Whig ministers, "I did not care if they were all hanged." Rather than one of indifference, Swift's mood was one of active animosity against the Whig politicians who, he felt, had used him shabbily, and of cautious receptivity toward the Tories, whose principles he admired and whose blandishments he was now prepared to receive.

Swift was forty-two years old when he arrived in London in 1710 for what he imagined would be a rather brief stay. He had been born in Dublin on November 30, 1667, only a few months after the death of his father. The elder Jonathan Swift had been one of the five sons of Thomas Swift, a staunchly royalist parson who had lost his living in Hertfordshire under Cromwell. All five sons sought their fortunes in Ireland, the only conspicuous success coming to Godwin, through whose help young Jonathan received his education at the Kilkenny School and at Trinity College, Dublin. Early in 1689 Swift's stay at college was abruptly ended by a combination of his Uncle Godwin's failing fortunes and the political troubles which Trinity College (as a center of Irish Protestantism) was then facing. Shortly after leaving Trinity, Swift was able to obtain the modest post of secretary to Sir William Temple, one-time ambassador to The Hague and personal friend to William III. As Swift evinced his abilities, the duties he was called upon to perform for Temple grew in significance and interest, and there developed the beginnings of a friendship with his employer that lasted until Sir William's death. At Temple's estate in England, Moor Park, Swift also first met Esther Johnson—then only eight—who was to become the famous Stella of his later life.

After a little more than a year at Moor Park, Swift, already beginning to suffer the attacks of "giddiness" and deafness which plagued him all his life, left his position with Temple and returned to Ireland. Despite letters of introduction Temple had given him, Swift found no means of livelihood in Ireland, and in the autumn of 1691, he returned to England; only a few months later Swift once more entered the employ of Sir William, but this time his position at Moor Park was on a higher level than before. Temple now treated the young man with greater respect and confidence, and frequently trusted him with affairs of importance. His increased contact with men in government and with national politics produced mixed reactions in Swift. The fixed lines of political opinion, the rejection of individuality often necessary in public life, and the pettiness of so many politicians, he found repelling. The excitement, the drama, and the feeling of power and influence involved in politics, however, strongly attracted him.

Swift's political connections through Temple were with the Whigs, whose animosity toward James II and whose fears over his possible return, Swift, as an Anglo-Irish Protestant, naturally shared—though Swift's High Church conservatism kept him from any very fervent espousal of general Whig policies. While perfectly willing and even anxious to seek preferment through his Whig connections, Swift in his early political allegiance seems on the whole to have been attracted rather to individual Whig politicians than to the Whig cause. Knowing that his employment at Moor Park could last only as long as the aging Temple survived, Swift renewed his earlier determination to achieve independence from Sir William and to attain a career of his own. His training, background, and connections caused him to turn to the Church. In May, 1694, he left Moor Park and went to Ireland, where in 1695 he was ordained and given the living of Kilroot, near Belfast. The living was a rural one, and the congregation was small. After the exciting bustle of Moor Park, the placid country atmosphere in Kilroot began to pall very quickly. When Swift had last left Temple's employ, a coolness had arisen between them, but now Sir William wrote, inviting the young man to return, and Swift gladly did so.

Swift's life at Moor Park came to a close in 1699 when Sir William died, leaving the task of editing his works to his young friend. These works, in five volumes, appeared separately between 1700 and 1709. The first to be published—one of three volumes of Temple's letters—Swift dedicated to King William in hopes of receiving thereby some preferment. The effort did not succeed, and Swift, considerably disappointed, obtained the position of secretary and chaplain to Lord Berkeley, through whose influence and help he was in 1700 given the livings of Laracor, Agher, and Rathbeggan in Meath, thus achieving his independence.

In April of 1701 Swift returned with Berkeley to England. At this time the first of Swift's political pamphlets appeared. Published, as the practice went, anonymously, it was called *On the Contests and Dissensions at Athens and Rome.* Party feeling in England was, as usual, running high, and Robert Harley, Tory Speaker of the House, had introduced a resolution to impeach the late Whig ministers. The Tories controlled Commons, but Harley's resolution was defeated in the Whig House of Lords. The pamphlet, which achieved some popularity, placed Swift on the Whig side, and so, ironically, in his first appearance as a political pamphleteer, Swift found himself in opposition to his later friend and patron, Harley. When, in September, 1701, on the death of James II, Louis XIV recognized the Pretender, King William was once more hailed as England's Protestant savior, and the Tories were discredited and defeated at the polls. Proud of his pamphlet's close forecast of events, Swift admitted his authorship of *Contests and Dissensions,* an avowal which won him his first taste of fame and helped secure him the friendship of Lord Somers, Bishop Burnet, and other prominent Whigs.

In November, 1703, Swift was back in England, where the Tories had once again achieved a political majority. A subject of major debate was the recurrent question of occasional conformity—that practice through which Dissenters received token Church of England communion once a year as a means of evading the Sacramental Test Act that had been designed to exclude them from public office. Only the year before, in

1702, a bill to bar occasional conformity had been rejected by Parliament, and now a similar bill, passed enthusiastically by Commons, was meeting strong opposition in Lords—opposition which eventually defeated it. Swift had little sympathy for occasional conformity, which in a few years he would publicly attack, but his connections with the Whigs led him at this time to oppose, albeit half-heartedly, the bill outlawing it. By June, 1704, when he returned to Laracor, Swift was suffering increased misgivings over the good faith of the Whigs' professed friendliness toward the Established Church, and though he remained nominally a Whig, he was not really in harmony with either party.

Before leaving London, Swift in 1704 published a volume containing his *Battle of the Books,* a short *Discourse on the Mechanical Operation of the Spirit,* and the work he had begun seven years before, the *Tale of a Tub.* Though the volume appeared anonymously, Swift was known by many to be its author, and his reputation as a writer grew. The *Tale of a Tub,* though in no way a partisan Whig tract, was dedicated to Lord Somers, and the ridicule which the book directed at certain Tories helped make its author more welcome in Whig circles. The book's reception by Queen Anne was less successful. Her widely-shared opinion that the book was blasphemous was reputedly instrumental in Swift's later difficulties in his search for advancement within the Church.

In April of 1705, Swift, now a man of some literary fame, once more came to visit London. In the seesaw battle of party politics, the Whigs were again rising in power, and Swift was in close contact with the prominent leaders of the party, as well as with its literary lights. At Will's Coffee House his friendship with his old school friend, William Congreve, was renewed, and he also became the friend of Joseph Addison, Samuel Garth, Ambrose Philips, Matthew Prior, Richard Steele, and others. Swift was careless as to the fortunes of his works, seemingly indifferent to their reception, and not clearly known as the author of many of them—all qualities which recommended him to the Whig literary circle as a man who was a brother wit, but not a rival.

The victories Marlborough had only recently won at Blenheim, Ramillies, and Turin encouraged England to continue the War of the Spanish Succession, and peace overtures made by the French king in 1706 were rejected. The Whigs met scarcely any opposition to their plan to pursue the war. In Parliament's session during early 1707 the question of union with Scotland was pressed. The Tories opposed the Whig plan for a union, and since most Anglicans were suspicious of union with Presbyterians, by their stand the Tories won further support among Churchmen. Tory opposition did not succeed in stopping the bill for union from passing, but the opposition did attract Church sympathizers, among them Swift, whose comments, as recorded in his "Verses Said to be Written on the Union" (1707), make his disapproval clear:

> Whoever yet a Union saw
> Of Kingdoms, without Faith or Law.
> Henceforward let no Statesman dare,
> A Kingdom to a Ship compare;
> Lest he should call our Commonweal,
> A Vessel with a double Keel:
> Which just like ours, new rigg'd and man'd,
> And got about a League from Land,
> By Change of Wind to Leeward Side
> The Pilot knew not how to guide.
> So tossing Faction will o'erwhelm
> Our crazy double-bottom'd Realm.[2]

Despite Swift's growing disenchantment, in 1707, when Archbishop King of the Irish Church was looking for an agent to approach the Whig ministry in an effort to win remission of the First Fruits and Twentieth Parts, the Vicar of Laracor seemed a natural choice. Swift's High Church sympathies, his considerable, if somewhat scandalous, literary fame, and his acquaintance with prominent figures in the Whig hierarchy all combined to recommend him for the task. Among Swift's personal motives for accepting the commission were his still bright hopes for preferment in the Church, specifically for the vacant bishopric of Waterford. Accordingly, in November, 1707, Swift once again set out for London and the political arena.

The term "First Fruits" had in feudal times referred to the first year's income, which it was customary for recipients of benefices to pay to the Pope in return for his patronage. Under the reforms of Henry VIII in England, the First Fruits reverted to the king, but in 1703–4 Queen Anne established a trust fund under which First Fruit payments were used in the Church of England for the augmentation of poor Church livings. The queen had likewise agreed to remit payment of the Twentieth Parts—the traditional papal tax of one twentieth of the annual income of a benefice, which after the Reformation had been annexed to the Crown. The Whig ministers had hoped that the bestowal of these much-desired remissions would soften Church opposition to such Whig-sponsored measures as occasional conformity. The English Church, though without showing any perceptible relaxation in its disapproval of Dissenters, had accepted the First Fruits and Twentieth Parts, and now the Irish Church was anxious to enjoy equivalent grants.

In London, Swift directed his petition to Sidney, Earl of Godolphin, the lord treasurer, who, beginning as a moderate Tory, had while in office emerged as a Whig. Between Swift and Godolphin there arose an immediate personal antipathy—an antipathy made all the more deep on Swift's side by Godolphin's hints that only by giving up the Sacramental Test Act could the Irish Church hope to receive the First Fruits. For almost two years Swift remained in England pressing his efforts on behalf of his Church and his own hopes for the bishopric of Waterford. In June of 1709, disappointed on both scores, he returned to Laracor and his vicarage.

In the summer of 1710 when the Irish Church decided to renew its request for the First Fruits, it once more turned to Swift as a petitioner on its behalf. His personal resentment toward the Whigs and his increased distrust of their policies toward the Church had by now led Swift to assume a political attitude which, while ostensibly neutral, in reality left him well prepared to welcome the discreet overtures the Tory ministry was shortly to make. The political scene that greeted Swift in England in 1710 was quite different from the one he had left behind after his earlier unsuccessful effort to win his Church the First Fruits. During his 1707–9 visit Swift had found the Whigs solidly entrenched, still enjoying the popularity produced by Marlborough's military victories on the Continent. By the fall of 1710, however, the burdens of the war were being felt more and more, as prices rose and scarcity began to spread. Louis XIV's successful appeal to his people, after his earlier peace overtures had been rejected by the Whig ministry, had strengthened the French war effort, while discontent over the seemingly endless conflict was rising in England.

Whig popularity also suffered from the surprising and arrogant request from Marlborough to the queen that he be made captain-general for life.

Though the request was refused, it had shocked the nation, and Tory pamphleteers were never to allow Marlborough to forget it. It was at this time, too, in the months before the opening of Parliament in November, 1709, that the extremist High Churchman, Dr. Henry Sacheverell, renewed his violent denunciations of all Dissenters. His fanatical sermons were distasteful to moderate Churchmen, but the Whig ministers, seeing a chance to get at the Church party, which they felt was partly responsible for their waning power, decided to prosecute Sacheverell. Under the prodding of Godolphin, to whom Sacheverell had referred contemptuously, Commons resolved to impeach the clergyman for high crimes and misdemeanors. This prosecution alarmed the nation, and Sacheverell, who was given a three-year suspension, became a popular hero. The Whig ministry had alienated the sympathies of the nation by its handling of this incident. For Swift, it was yet another impetus for his approaching break with the Whigs.

In the autumn of 1710, Swift came to an England that was weary of the war, and where angry mobs toasted Sacheverell and denounced the Whigs. During the previous summer Swift had hinted at the possibility of the shift which he was shortly to make. In a letter to Benjamin Tooke, his bookseller in London, Swift wrote that he had new plans of work, and would soon come to England, "since it is like to be a new world, and since I have the merit of suffering by not complying with the old." [3] The first step toward toppling the Whig ministry had been the removal in June of the Earl of Sunderland. The weakening Whigs sought aid among the wealthy, who feared a collapse of credit if Godolphin withdrew from office, and from the Allies, who feared England's withdrawal from the war. But popular sentiment had become strongly anti-Whig, and in August steps to dissolve Parliament and ask the verdict of the public were taken. By the time Swift came to London in September, Godolphin had been removed, and Harley had been taken into the Privy Council and named chancellor of the exchequer. The Whigs had fallen, and the "new world" Swift mentioned had arrived.

Swift's stay in England was to last, with one interruption, until August of 1714, and the "journal" he faithfully wrote to Stella for the first three of these years records his transformation into a Tory stalwart. When he arrived, Swift seemed concerned only with accomplishing his mission on behalf of the Irish Church, and there was no sign yet of a political switch.

"The Whigs were ravished to see me, and would lay hold on me as a twig while they are drowning . . ." (*Stella*, I, 5), he wrote on September 9, 1710. For the moment, Swift continued to associate with Addison, Congreve, Steele, and other Whig authors, and even wrote a brief, nonpolitical piece for the *Tatler*.[4]

As time wore on, however, he became increasingly estranged from the Whigs. Almost immediately upon arrival in London he had gone to see Godolphin concerning the petition for the First Fruits. Godolphin's coolness had left Swift angry and disgruntled. His letters to Stella reveal that at first he seemingly had no intention of joining the Tories, but rather fancied himself in the role of an impartial spectator to politics. The Tories, however, were anxious to have Swift's pen working in their behalf, and they courted his support. On September 30, he writes to Stella: "The Tories dryly tell me, I may make my fortune, if I please; but I do not understand them, or rather, I do understand them" (I, 36).

Harley realized that Swift could not be approached with crude offers of money or advancement. To a man who burned with resentment over what he felt was personal neglect by the Whigs, the most effective appeal was one of cordial friendship and respect. As opposed to Godolphin's cold and condescending formality, Harley and St. John offered an easy social equality and a flattering receptivity to Swift's opinions and suggestions. As Swift's correspondence indicates, by August, 1710, he had discarded the Whigs. He revenged himself for Godolphin's cool reception by publishing early in October the *Virtues of Sid Hamet, the Magician's Rod*, a lampoon ridiculing the deposed minister. By November 2, two months after his arrival in England, Swift's new political identification was complete, and on that day, in the *Examiner*, he made his first appearance in the role of defender and spokesman of the Tory ministry's campaign to terminate the War of the Spanish Succession.

II

Swift's hostile biographers of the eighteenth and early nineteenth centuries (see, for example, Thackeray's *English Humourists*) have so often pictured his political conversion as an ignoble act of pure opportunism that it is worth taking time here to re-examine the nature of Swift's political principles and his early association with Whiggism. In the late seventeenth century the very concept of political parties was ill-defined, and it is unlikely that Swift, prior to his employment with Sir William Temple, would have firmly aligned himself with either political party. As a High Church adherent and a man whose grandfather had suffered under the Commonwealth for his royalist loyalties, Swift had both family tradition and personal sympathies of Tory rather than Whig tendency, though as a member of the Anglo-Irish Protestant minority in a predominantly Catholic country, Swift subscribed to the anti-Romanism most closely identified with the Whig cause. The commitment Swift was to make to Whiggism was at its best a tepid thing compared to his later fervent Toryism, and it is difficult not to think that his original identification in the Whig interest was largely due to the fortuitous circumstance that Sir William Temple happened to be a Whig rather than a Tory politician. It was only natural that Temple's ambitious young secretary should assume something of the political coloration of the man upon whom he was dependent for his livelihood and hopes for advancement. In his years at Moor Park, Swift met King William and many prominent Whig statesmen. A young clergyman anxious to make his way in the Church could not easily afford to ignore such valuable connections, and thus both chance and expediency worked initially to bind Swift to the Whig party.

Although self-interest was no less present in Swift's motives than in those of most men, to suggest that deep political conviction played only a subsidiary role in his early identification as a Whig is not to accuse him of pure and simple self-seeking. In Temple's brand of cautious and philosophical Whiggism, there was nothing of a kind to repel the young Swift, nor did he ever in his career as a Whig endorse any principles widely at variance with his later Toryism. Swift's correspondence up to his conversion in 1710 reveals him as a person in whose life politics, except in matters of religion, played no central role. Despite his nominal Whiggism, he seldom expresses any emphatic political opinions, and the general tone of Swift's pre-1710 letters is that of a man not deeply involved in political concerns. Even when he deals with explicitly political matters, his Whiggism is distinctly lukewarm. In certain of his early poems, as in the *Ode to King William* (1690), Swift expresses mild antiroyal-prerogative (hence, Whiggish) sentiments, but his only political tract written for the Whigs, *A Discourse on the Contests and Dissensions in*

Athens and Rome (1701), enunciates a balance-of-power policy based upon principles which are neither distinctly Whig nor Tory. The *Battle of the Books* and *Tale of a Tub* (written *ca.* 1697), insofar as they are political at all, suggest no clear partisan allegiance beyond a general philosophical and literary conservatism. In his later series of tracts on Church affairs, of which the most important are *Project for the Advancement of Religion* (1709), *Sentiments of a Church-of-England Man* (1708), and *Letter Concerning the Sacramental Test* (1708), Swift assumes a more distinctly High Church posture, which is by implication Tory.[5]

If, as I have suggested, chance and expediency played a considerable part in Swift's identification as a Whig, it is greatly to the credit of his consistency that at no time during his career as a Whig did he try to hide his generally High Church principles. To an obscure young Churchman seeking favor from powerful Whig lords there would have been much advantage in altering or at least concealing High Church sympathies. High Church Whigs, though by no means unheard of, were something of an anomaly, and were unlikely to achieve much in the way of preferment. Yet, in his first piece of political writing, *Ode to Dr. William Sancroft* (1692), Swift assumes the High Church position he was never to relinquish:

> Some angel say, what were the nation's crimes,
> That sent these wild reformers to our times;
> Say what their senseless malice meant,
> To tear Religion's lovely face;
> Strip her of ev'ry ornament and grace,
> In striving to wash off th'imaginary paint.
> (*Poems*, I, 42)

The general looseness of Swift's commitment to Whig principles, as evidenced most particularly in his professed High Church convictions, may well have contributed to his failure to win any advancement from the Whig lords he solicited. When in 1708 the *Letter Concerning the Sacramental Test* was published, Archbishop King, Swift's superior in Dublin, was amazed that a nominal "Whig" could have written it. "But pray," King writes to Swift on February 10, 1708, "by what artifice did you contrive to pass for a Whig? As I am an honest man, I courted the greatest Whigs I knew, and could not gain the reputation of being counted one" (*Correspondence, I,* 123).

But if Swift's Whiggism was of a superficial sort, before 1710 it was as a Whig that his contemporaries viewed him and that he sought his personal advancement. The same Archbishop King who expressed astonishment that a Whig could have written the *Letter Concerning the Sacramental Test* was instrumental in selecting Swift as a suitable emissary to the Whig ministry for the Irish Church in its attempts to win the First Fruits. In 1707 and 1710 it was Swift's access to prominent Whigs and his presumed favor with them that brought him this commission, as is indicated by the fact that when the Godolphin ministry fell in 1710, the Irish bishops immediately considered recalling him. Archbishop King writes Swift on November 2, 1710: "I am not to conceal from you, that some [of the Irish bishops] expressed a little jealousy that you would not be acceptable to the present courtiers, intimating that you were under the reputation of being a favourite of the late party in power" (*Correspondence, I,* 189). One can easily imagine how ironically King's letter, written on the very day that the newly converted Swift made his first appearance as a Tory pamphleteer in the *Examiner,* must have read to its recipient. The irony was doubled when Swift's letter announcing his success in the matter of the First Fruits was crossed in the mails by the letter from King relieving him of his commission.

To argue that Swift was never a Whig in any profound sense does not necessarily imply that his motives when he did make his switch to Toryism were particularly lofty ones. If chance and expediency were the major factors that had led him to ally himself with the Whigs, the same elements played a considerable role in his conversion to the Tory cause—the difference being that, as a High Churchman and a conservative, he could embrace Tory principles with an enthusiasm and sincerity he was never able to muster on behalf of the Whigs. To many students of Swift, his frequently expressed bitterness over his failure to win advancement with the Whigs has seemed, in view of the fact that the services he rendered them were few and equivocal, to be exaggerated and unjustified. However, Swift's disappointment was not so much in proportion to what he had done as it was to the promises which had been made to him. On October 6, 1709, Lord Halifax wrote to Swift, saying:

I am ashamed for my selfe and my Friends to see you left in a Place, so incapable of tasting you, and to see so much Merit, and so great Qualitys unrewarded by those who are sensible of them. Mr Addison and I are enter'd into a New Confederacy, never to give over the pursuit, nor to cease reminding those, who can serve you, till your worth is placed in that light where it ought to shine. [*Correspondence,* I, 150]

On the margin of this letter, in Swift's hand, there appears the significant comment, "I kept this lett^r as a true Original of Courtiers & Court promises."

Thwarted personal ambition, however, cannot in itself fully explain the anger Swift felt toward the Whig ministers. The Tories, in their turn, were to be just as free with lavish promises of advancement, and since Swift's contribution to the Tory cause was of crucial importance, he could have, with far more justice than in the case of the Whigs, accused Harley of insufficient gratitude. Yet he never did so, and in later life, though he professed to scorn all politicians and courtiers, his expressions of disappointment over this betrayal of his hopes are remarkably free of bitterness. The thing that seems to have galled him most in the treatment he received from the Whigs is their failure to respect his sense of his own dignity and self-respect. To be treated as an underling, to be received in a manner indicating indifference or contempt, to be taken for granted— these were things quite intolerable to Swift's fierce pride: ". . . my lord treasurer [Godolphin] received me with a great deal of coldness," Swift writes to Stella on September 9, 1710, "which has enraged me so, I am almost vowing revenge" (I, 6). The man who had so resented Sir William Temple's coldness was particularly touchy on matters of the treatment he received from the great, and it is in this light that we must view Swift's sense of personal grievance and his desire for "revenge" against the deposed Whig ministry.

Had Swift been a mere time-server, he would surely, upon his arrival in London in 1710, have made overtures to the new ministry; but the *Journal to Stella* and his correspondence for the period show clearly that it was the ministry which broached the subject of conversion. From his first meeting with Swift, on October 4, 1710—when Swift in his official capacity presented the Irish Church's petition for the First Fruits—Harley began his efforts to recruit Swift to the Tory cause. That Swift may not at first have been altogether amenable to conversion is suggested by the scorn with which, only a week before his initial meeting with Harley, he describes the flock of ex-Whigs suddenly turned Tory. On September 26, 1710, in a letter to Dean Stearne, Swift writes:

The Whigs, like an army beat three quarters out of the field, begin to skirmish but faintly; and deserters daily come over. We are amazed to find our mistakes, and how it was possible to see so much merit where there was none, and to overlook it where there was so much. When a great Minister has lost his place, immediately virtue, honour, and wit, fly over to his successor, with the other ensigns of his office. [*Correspondence,* I, 178]

That part of Swift's irony in this letter is self-directed is indicated by his use of "we" when speaking of the disenchanted Whigs. And Swift finally made the decision which his principles, personal ambitions, and motives of revenge all dictated only after he had been subjected to a month-long campaign of Harley's blandishments.

In the eighteenth century, as in our own, it was altogether natural that a man in Swift's position should hope to use his political connections as a means to further his own career. For a clergyman of modest birth, patronage from the great was not only the most reliable method of advancement, it was almost the only one. Thus, it in no way reflects upon the sincerity of Swift's commitment to the Tory ministry that he hoped for some preferment as a reward for his services. As a proud man, he scorned the money payment Harley was once so indiscreet as to offer him, and this despite his frequent complaints in the *Journal to Stella* that the meagerness of his income made it difficult for him to keep up with his new friends among the great. But the same pride which led him indignantly to refuse a salary kept him from personally pressing his claim to preferment. On September 1, 1711, when Swift was completing his first year as a Tory pamphleteer, Archbishop King wrote from Dublin:

I promised to say something as to your own affairs; and the first thing is, not to neglect yourself on this occasion, but to make use of the favour and interest you have at present to procure you some preferment that may be called a settlement. Years come on, and after a certain age, if a man be not in a station that may be a step to a better, he seldom goes higher. It is with men as with beauties, if they pass the flower, they grow stale, and lie for ever neglected. I know you are not ambitious; but it is prudence, not ambition, to get into a station, that may make a man easy, and prevent contempt when he grows in years. You certainly may now have an opportunity to provide for yourself, and I entreat you not to neglect it. [*Correspondence,* I, 254]

To this admonition to look after his self-interest, Swift replied on October 1, 1711:

As to . . . my Fortune, I shall never be able to make myself believed how indifferent I am about it. I sometimes have the Pleasure of making that of others; and, I fear it is too great a Pleasure to be a Virtue, at least in me. Perhaps, in *Ireland,* I may not be able to prevent Contempt any other Way than by making my Fortune; but, then it is my Comfort, that Contempt in *Ireland* will be no Sort of Mortification to me. . . . I am as well received and known at Court, as perhaps any man ever was of my Level; I have formerly been the like. I left it then, and will perhaps leave it now (when they please to let me) without any Concern, but what a few Months will remove. . . . I never will solicit for myself, although I often do for others. [*Correspondence,* I, 262]

The *Journal to Stella* confirms Swift's assertion that he refused to solicit for advancement on his own behalf, but this does not mean, as he loftily suggests to his ecclesiastical superior, that he was indifferent to his fortunes; though pride might keep him from petitioning in person, it did not preclude a natural interest and concern in the matter. Shortly after joining the Tories he writes to Stella: "Perhaps they may be just as grateful as others: but, according to the best judgment I have, they are pursuing the true interest of the public; and therefore I am glad to contribute what is in my power" (I, 108). Yet four months later, Swift ends on a less altruistic tone, as he tells Stella:

I did not expect to find such friends as I have done. They may indeed deceive me too. But there are important reasons . . . why they should not. . . . The assurances they give me, without any scruple or provocation, are such as are usually believed in the world; they may come to nothing, but the first opportunity that offers, and is neglected, I shall depend no more, but come away. [I, 233]

Nevertheless, it was three years after the above was written before Swift was to "come away," even though he had meanwhile been by-passed in the filling of more than one desirable Church vacancy. As time passed, Swift seems to have become less hopeful regarding his chances for preferment, and he sought by his pessimism to prepare himself for disappointment, telling Stella, "Remember if I am used ill and ungratefully, as I have formerly been, 'tis what I am prepared for, and shall not wonder at it" (I, 303). To suggest that the primary motive behind Swift's allegiance to the Tory ministry was hope of personal gain is, as I have earlier remarked, to overlook the relative absence of rancor he evidenced when his reward proved to be negligible: the deanery of St. Patrick's which he finally obtained was little more than he might have expected without devoting himself to four years of pamphleteering. "I loved My Lord Your father better than any other Man in the World," he writes to Harley's son in 1737, "although I had no obligation to him on the Score of Preferment, having been driven to this wretched Kingdom . . . by his want of power to keep me in what I ought to call my own Country" (*Correspondence,* V, 46). When, in the introduction to the *History of the Four Last Years of the Queen,* Swift tells his readers how little he received for his services, he does no more than list the facts: "I never received one shilling from the minister, or any other present, except that of a few books; nor did I want their assistance to support me. I very often indeed dined with the Treasurer and Secretary; but, in those days, that was not reckoned a bribe. . . ." [6]

There was, however, a less tangible reward, perhaps no less important to Swift than preferment, that was amply forthcoming from Harley and St. John: gratification of his sense of pride and self-respect which had been so long starved under the Whigs. After the coldness of Godolphin and the other Whigs, Harley's easy intimacy and the obvious high value he and St. John placed upon Swift's genius were of considerable appeal in winning Swift over. The pleasure Swift took in being treated as an equal by the ministers of state is apparent throughout the *Journal to Stella,* as is his touchiness and immediate response to any signs of aloofness on their part. On October 14, 1710, he writes to Stella:

I suppose I have said enough in this and a former letter [of] how I stand with [the] new people; ten times better than ever I did with the old; forty times more caressed. I am to dine to-morrow at Mr. Harley's; and if he continues as he has begun, no man has been ever better treated by another. [I, 58–59]

With minor lapses, both Harley and St. John continued to be as solicitous of Swift's stubborn pride as if they had been the courtiers and he the great lord. On one occasion, after St. John had behaved with uncharacteristic formality toward him, Swift responded with a rebuke which bears quotation at length:

. . . one thing I warned him of, Never to appear cold to me, for I would not be treated like a school-boy; that I had felt too much of that in my life already (meaning from sir William Temple); that I expected every great minister, who honoured me with his acquaintance, if he heard or saw any thing to my disadvantage, would let me know it in plain words, and not put me in pain to guess by the change or coldness of his countenance or behaviour; for it was what I would hardly bear from a crowned head, and I thought no subject's favour was worth it; and that I designed to let my lord keeper and Mr. Harley know the same thing, that they might use me accordingly. He took all right; said, I had reason, vowed nothing ailed him but sitting up whole nights at business . . . ; would have had me dine with him . . . to make up matters; but I would not. I don't know, but I would not. [*Stella,* I, 230]

These are not the words or actions of a man overwhelmingly anxious to ingratiate himself in hopes of preferment.

The published views that Swift expressed in his role as a Tory political propagandist were, in the nature of the situation, not always an exact reflection of his personal opinion. Any rhetorician, if he remains steadily aware of his audience and his aims, will find that his task obliges him in one degree or another to suppress doubts, to simulate enthusiasm or indignation, to be carefully selective in his evidence, or in any of a hundred other ways to write what he thinks will best succeed in persuading. If we compare the opinions expressed in Swift's political tracts with the private opinions he records in his correspondence and in the *Journal to Stella,* it is not difficult to find cases in which his personal views are at variance with his published ones. However much Swift may have despised the Earl of Wharton, he evidently felt some misgivings over the mixture of rumors, half-truths, and libels he included in the scurrilous "character" of that lord which he published. Although he usually took no particular pains to conceal from Stella his authorship of various tracts, when the *Character of Wharton* appeared, he wrote: "Here's a damned libellous pamphlet come out against lord Wharton, giving the character first, and then telling some of his actions: the character is very well, but the facts indifferent" (I, 115). Again regarding the same pamphlet, he tells her,

"The character is here reckoned admirable, but most of the facts are trifles" (I, 148).

In the case of the Duke of Marlborough there is a discrepancy between the line taken by Swift in print and his opinion as expressed privately. Marlborough, when Swift began writing for the Tories, was a towering military hero, though his decline in popularity had already begun. To discredit Marlborough and hasten that decline was an important aspect of Swift's job. Thus, in his role as a propagandist, Swift did not hesitate to belittle Marlborough's record as a general, to imply that he was a personal coward, to suggest that he had ambitions for the throne, and to accuse him of prolonging the war to enrich himself. Yet, typical of Swift's remarks on Marlborough in the *Journal to Stella* is his comment:

> I think our friends press a little too hard on the duke of Marlborough. . . . I question whether ever any wise state laid aside a general who had been successful nine years together, whom the enemy so much dread; and his own soldiers cannot but believe must always conquer; and you know that in war opinion is nine parts in ten. [I, 159]

Examples of this sort could be multiplied, as in the matter of Swift's unqualified praise of the queen in print versus his exasperation with her in private,* or as in the contrast between his published and private views on such matters as the October Club and the High Flier doctrine of passive obedience.

To demonstrate such discrepancies of opinion between Swift, the private citizen, and Swift, the Tory pamphleteer, however, is not to discover any special cynicism in his political tracts. In purely ethical terms, of course, any falsification of one's feelings is more or less reprehensible, and to a large extent the modern disrepute of the very words "rhetoric" and "propaganda" springs from the reader's sense that a man seeking to persuade will often sacrifice strict truth for expediency. Nevertheless, it is permissible and necessary, in terms of his purpose, that a propagandist

---

* See the *Journal to Stella,* December 8–29, 1711. When the House of Lords passed the Earl of Nottingham's resolution insisting that no part of Spain be ceded to the House of Bourbon, it looked for a time as if the Tory ministry would topple. On this occasion Swift (who in his public writings always portrayed the queen as fully supporting Harley and St. John) blamed the queen, characterizing her as "false" and speaking of her "betrayal" of the ministry.

occasionally oversimplify a problem or show confidence where he feels none. This is not to say that the propagandist has license to indulge in gross distortion or dishonesty, but merely that he is allowed to place his case in the best possible light. The difference between Swift's published and private opinions may do some damage to his pretenses as a "historian," but they do not make him guilty, except in a limited ethical sense, of cynicism. Indeed, these differences—adding up, as they do, to a rather paltry list of minor points—furnish considerable evidence for Swift's sincerity, for seldom in the vast bulk of his public writings is there any major instance where Swift wrote what he believed to be basically false.

As I have tried to show, the element of opportunism, while by no means absent, was not the primary factor which led Swift to ally himself with the Tories. His initial allegiance to the Whigs seems to have derived not so much from deep conviction as from a combination of his early connections with Temple and a certain sympathy—natural in an Anglo-Irish Protestant in the 1680's—toward the party most solicitous about the Protestant Succession. Among the Whigs his High Church sympathies had always made him a kind of misfit, and when Harley's overtures paved the way for him to enter the party toward which his principles had always inclined, he did so. To be sure, it was a choice strongly supported by motives of revenge, vanity, and hope of gain, but this does not detract from the fact that his conversion in no way violated his basic convictions. It could, indeed, be argued that if there is some tincture of opportunism in Swift's political career, it is to be found rather in his acceptance for so long of the uncongenial role of Whig than in his eventual emergence as a Tory.

III

The Tory ministers who had recruited Swift to their cause in 1710 realized that their control of the country depended upon how well they presented their case to the public, and for this task no better man than Swift could be found. Weariness over the war was deepening. Heavy taxes had injured trade, bankruptcies were common, recruits were scarce, and many farms were tenantless. These signs all pointed toward the desirability of a quick peace, and so it was to this end that the ministry applied itself and toward which Swift gave his invaluable aid. The opposition of the Whigs and the Allies to the ending of the war was formidable, and the early peace negotiations were carried on in secret. The news that the Tories were actively seeking to negotiate a peace soon leaked out, however, and the already vehement controversy carried on in periodicals, pamphlets, and broadsides by Whig and Tory propagandists reached a new pitch of intensity.

Swift's political writings on behalf of the Tory ministry may be divided roughly into three groups, each having a slightly different objective. Swift's first compositions for the Tories, such works as the *Examiner* papers (1710–11) and the scurrilous *Short Character of His Excellency Thomas Earl of Wharton* (1710), have as their primary goal the discrediting of the Whig leaders and their policies. Once this task had been successfully accomplished, Swift directed his efforts toward producing a climate of opinion favorable to the abandonment of England's Dutch allies and the conclusion of the war. To this end he wrote such works as the *Conduct of the Allies* (1711), *Some Remarks on the Barrier Treaty* (1712), and the *Letter to a Whig Lord* (1712). Once the Peace of Utrecht had been ratified, Swift's primary task became to defend the peace against the accusations of betrayal leveled by the Whigs and the Dutch; this defense Swift offered in such works as the *History of the Four Last Years of the Queen* (1713—not published until 1758), *Importance of the "Guardian" Considered* (1713), and *Publick Spirit of the Whigs* (1714).

The exact nature of the role played by Swift in the Harley–St. John ministry is a question over which his critics and biographers have widely differed. Bernard Acworth, who sees Swift's position as one of tremendous power and influence, goes so far as to say, "During this period [1710–14] Swift may almost be said to have ruled England and, indeed, Europe, where everything revolved round the War which had dragged on since 1701."[7] To others Swift appears as a dupe, a man flatteringly cultivated by politicians anxious for the services of his pen, but given only such minimal information and power as would increase his effectiveness as a propagandist. As the Earl of Orrery puts it:

He was elated with the appearance of enjoying ministerial confidence. He enjoyed the shadow: the substance was detained from him. He was employed, not trusted; and at the same time that he imagined himself a subtil diver, who dextrously shot down into the profoundest regions of politics, he was suffered only to sound the shallows nearest the shore, and was scarce admitted to descend below the froth at the top. Perhaps the deeper bottoms were too muddy for his inspection.[8]

It is impossible today to say with certainty whether Swift was a wielder of tremendous power in the Harley–St. John ministry or merely a tool, but either of these two views is apt to be damaging to Swift—for if his knowledge of the ministry's affairs was merely superficial, then his pretense in the larger political tracts to be writing from a full knowledge of all that went on is exploded; on the other hand, if he was privy to all the affairs of the ministry, then he stands to some degree implicated in Harley and St. John's negotiations with the Pretender. There is no reason, however, not to accept (albeit with certain reservations) Swift's own balanced view of his importance in the Tory ministry. In his *Memoirs Relating to That Change Which Happened in the Queen's Ministry in the Year 1710* (1714), Swift opens by saying:

Having continued, for near the space of four years, in a good degree of confidence with the ministry then in being, though not with so much power as was believed, or at least given out, by my friends as well as my enemies . . . : And this having happened during a very busy period of negotiations abroad, and management or intrigue at home, I thought it might probably, some years hence . . . be an entertainment to those who will have any personal regard for me or my memory, to set down some particularities which fell under my knowledge and observation. . . . [*Prose Works,* VIII, 107]

It will be noticed that Swift specifically denies that he was a power in the ministry, claiming no more than moderate intimacy with the ministers and an observation post near the center of events.

Although Harley and St. John's candor with Swift was less than he supposed, there seems to be little doubt that in most matters he did enjoy "a good degree of confidence" from them. In his position as chief Tory propagandist, Swift was obliged to argue the ministry's case before the public, and it was therefore important that he be well informed, at least in general terms, as to the ministry's goals and policies. Nor was Swift hesitant in asserting his rights in this matter. Regarding a social dinner he attended with the ministers, Swift writes Stella: "Ld Bol———— told me I must walk away to day when dinner was done, because Ld Tr and he and anothr [*sic*] were to enter on Business: but I sd it was as fit I should know their Business as any body; for I was to justify; so the rest went, and I stayd . . . ," though, as Swift dryly goes on to admit, "[the business discussed] was so important I was like to sleep over it" (II, 589). The *Journal to Stella* reveals that Harley and St. John did not usually have to be asked, as in the instance just quoted, to allow Swift to attend discussions of state affairs. More often it was at their flattering insistence that he was present at the meetings which furnished him with suggestions and ideas for his pamphlets. There is little doubt that, within the bounds of discretion, Harley and St. John actually did confide in Swift, for to admit Swift into their private counsels—although not to the most secret ones—was not only the best way to insure his loyalty but also a means of controlling the sort of information that he published. It became a matter of course with Swift to have all his tracts, with the exception of a few of the smaller ones, carefully perused by the ministers and corrected for "fact" before publication.

Swift's claim to the ministry's confidence is of particular interest with regard to his *Four Last Years of the Queen.* It is in this tract more than in any other that he tells us he used special sources not generally available. He presents himself as viewing the negotiations preliminary to the Peace of Utrecht from a position of a privileged insider with access to secret material. In his preface he says:

The materials for this History, besides what I have already mentioned, I mean the confidence reposed in me for those four years, by the chief persons in power, were extracted out of many hundred letters written by our ambassadors abroad, and from the answers as well as instructions sent to them by our Secretaries of state, or by the first minister the Earl of *Oxford.* The former were all originals, and the latter copies entered into books in the secretaries office, out of both which I collected all that I thought convenient; not to mention several memorials given me by the ministers at home. Further, I was a constant witness and observer of all that passed, and entered every particular of any consequence upon paper. [*Prose Works,* VII, xxxiv]

Swift's claim to special information is no rhetorical exaggeration, for Harley did in fact place at his disposal a vast number of secret letters and other documents, and there is every indication that Swift put them to careful use. While composing the *Four Last Years of the Queen,* he tells Stella: "I toil like a horse, and have hundreds of letters still to read; and squeeze a line perhaps out of each, or at least the seeds of a line" (II,

569). In support of Swift's claims, Sir Harold Williams has recently discovered in the Public Record Office secret documents of the Tory ministry concerning the peace negotiations. Examining such papers as the Preliminary Demands submitted to France by Prior in 1711, the French Response, and various others of a confidential nature, Williams found that Swift's text showed unmistakably that he had used these materials, and in one case at least, the document in question is clearly endorsed in Swift's own hand.[9]

However, such confidential information as Harley and St. John saw fit to entrust to Swift, while considerable, was far from complete. When the composition of his pamphlets or his own demands for respect as an equal made it desirable the ministers could allow Swift a glance at the inner workings of their administration. But both men independently carried on numerous intrigues which required absolute secrecy while in negotiation, and regarding such matters neither man could afford to confide in any outside person. So little was Swift aware of such hidden currents in the Tory ministry that, though a personal friend of both Harley and St. John, he was for a long time blind to the bitter personal rivalry which would help to hasten their downfall.

The most politically embarrassing skeleton concealed in the Harley–St. John closet was the matter of their secret negotiations toward placing the Pretender on the English throne. Inevitably, there has been much speculation as to whether Swift suspected this design. In all Swift's vast body of correspondence and writings, there is nothing to indicate that he ever had knowledge of any of the attempts by the ministers to tamper with the Protestant succession. Typical of his remarks on the subject is his statement in *Some Free Thoughts Upon the Present State of Affairs* (1714):

I have . . . been assured by a Person of some Consequence, that during a very near and Constant Familiarity with the great Men at Court for four Years past, he never could observe even in those Hours of Conversation where there is usually least Restraint, that one Word ever passed among them to shew a Dislike of the present Settlement, although they would sometimes lament that the false Representations of their's and the Kingdom's Enemies had made some Impressions in the Mind of the Successor. [*Prose Works*, VIII, 90–91]

To underline the point, Swift has written in the margin of the manuscript, "The Author means himself." There is no reason to doubt Swift's denial that he ever heard the ministers discuss an approach to the Pretender. The matter was not one either Harley or St. John would be likely to hint at, especially to Swift. How he would have responded had any such hint been made is indicated in a letter he wrote to Archbishop King in 1716. King had written Swift, mentioning a rumor that St. John, then in exile, might soon be pardoned and allowed to return to England if he would confess to his dealings with the Pretender. King went on to say that he hoped such a confession would not implicate Swift. Swift immediately replied, denying belief in St. John's guilt and declaring his own ignorance of any such affair, saying:

Had there been ever the least Overture or Intent of bringing in the Pretender during my Acquaintance with the Ministry, I think I must have been very stupid not to have pickt out some discoveryes or Suspicions; and tho I am not sure I should have turned Informer, yet I am sure I should have dropt some generall Cautions, and immediately have retired. [*Correspondence,* II, 238]

Had the ministers been negotiating with the Pretender, Swift would thus, in his own terms have had to be "very stupid" not to suspect what was going on. Yet the ministers *were* doing just that,[10] and since it is difficult to think of Jonathan Swift as either stupid or unperceptive, there have always been some who think that Swift surmised more than he was willing to admit.

As a clergyman of the Church of England, Swift thought of himself as a moderate occupying the religious middle ground between the extremes of Romanism on one hand and of a motley group of Dissenters, Deists, and atheists on the other. Potentially both groups were equally dangerous in Swift's view, but it was the Dissenters who gave most immediate cause for concern. After the bloodless revolution of 1688 and the Act of Settlement (passed with Harley's aid) insuring a Protestant succession, the threat to England from Catholicism seemed for the moment remote. The Dissenters, however, despite the considerable civil disabilities heaped upon them, were flourishing. When the Whigs warned of danger from the Pretender, it seemed to Swift that by whipping up hysteria over an all but dead dragon they were hoping to call attention away from the real and immediate threat, which lay in the growing power of the nonconformists. Whatever the virtues of Swift's analysis of the situation, he was, in modern terms, so much on the alert for danger from the left, that it is not surprising he paid relatively little attention to the threat on the right.

His Whig counterparts were spreading so many rumors and accusations he *knew* to be false that it was not hard for Swift, when they accused the Tory ministry of Jacobitism, to dismiss the charge as mere slander. If he entertained any vague suspicions on the subject, they were easily suppressed as he faced what he felt were more pressing problems. We can see such a process going on in Swift's discussion of passive obedience in *Examiner* 33. We know from the *Journal to Stella* and the correspondence that Swift had serious reservations over the extremist Tory position that denied the people any right to resist their monarch, however tyrannous. Not caring to defend this doctrine, Swift chose to insist that the whole controversy was irrelevant: ". . . [the Tories] see no Reason for entring upon so ungrateful a Subject, or raising Controversies upon it, as if we were in daily Apprehensions of *Tyranny* . . ." (*Prose Works,* III, 114). In fact, the question was by no means as academic as Swift suggests, but his own doubts on the subject evidently kept him from wishing to consider it very profoundly. It is conceivable that similar doubts concerning the ministry's relationship to the Pretender kept him from probing deeply lest his vague fears should find a tangible basis. But there is no evidence to suggest that he felt such misgivings in the first place, and to the end of his life, Swift seems to have continued to feel that the charge of Jacobitism against Harley and St. John was nothing more than another Whig libel.

IV

In later life, Swift was to look back upon the years 1710–14 as the high point of his career. Paradoxically, however, though his power and effectiveness in his role as a Tory man of letters were considerable, in his personal fortunes, as we have seen, he was to suffer many keen disappointments. His petition in 1710 for the First Fruits had been cordially received by Harley, who placed the matter before the queen. As a pious Anglican, the queen was well inclined toward this remission, and shortly afterward granted it. Swift was highly pleased at the success of his official mission and immediately wrote a letter announcing the victory to Archbishop King in Dublin. The Irish bishops who had commissioned Swift to seek the First Fruits had originally been in doubt as to whether a man whose past connections had been with the Whigs could successfully champion their cause before the new Tory ministry. Unaware of Swift's new political alignment and hearing of the surge in Tory popularity, the Irish bishops came to feel that their cause would be more likely to flourish in other hands. As was mentioned earlier, at the very time Swift's letter announcing the queen's compliance with his request traveled westward to Dublin, it was crossed in the mails by a letter from Archbishop King to Swift informing him that his Whig background disqualified him as a suitable agent and that further negotiations over the First Fruits were to be handled by the Duke of Ormonde, the lord lieutenant. When eventually the official announcement of the granting of the First Fruits was made in Dublin, it was Ormonde, rather than Swift, who was credited with having handled the affair.

Still more disappointment awaited Swift in the matter of his preferment in the Church. As the vicar of Laracor and Rathbeggan, rector of Agher, and prebend of Dunlavin, Swift, despite all his titles, received an annual income of little more than three hundred pounds. The style of life imposed upon him by his new friendships with lords made it difficult for Swift to live within his income. In the *Journal to Stella* Swift expresses his annoyance on the days when rain storms have obliged him to spend extra money for coaches and his pleasure on the occasions when invitations from friends have enabled him to spend a week without buying his own dinner. Swift was too proud to accept the money payment he might have received for his services to the ministry, but he justly felt that a Church living of some dignity and of sufficient income to allow him to live in or near London was due him. In May, 1711, he writes Stella: "To return without some mark of distinction would look extremely little; and I would likewise gladly be somewhat richer than I am" (I, 276). In the spring of 1712, the deanery of Wells was vacated, and later that year the see of Hereford became available. Swift had hopes for both these positions, but his political pamphleteering had won him powerful enemies as well as powerful friends, and in both cases the appointments went to others. Likewise, the queen, reputedly scandalized over the *Tale of a Tub,* was disinclined to see Swift rise in the Church hierarchy. By April, 1713, with the Peace of Utrecht already signed, Swift announced to Harley and St. John (by now the Earl of Oxford and Viscount Bolingbroke) that unless "something honourable" should come his way immediately, he would shortly return to Ireland. Through the efforts of Harley and the

Duke of Ormonde, Swift was at last awarded the deanery of St. Patrick's in Dublin, and in June of 1713 Swift embarked for Ireland.

By September, Swift was back in London, having been urgently summoned in the hope that he might be useful in helping to mediate the growing personal feud between Harley and St. John. With the signing of the Peace of Utrecht, the natural rivalry of the two men had reasserted itself, and the resultant maneuverings threatened to split the entire party asunder at its moment of triumph. Swift's efforts to reconcile the two men were in vain, and by July 27, 1714, Harley resigned his post, and St. John became the ruling power of the ministry. His glory was short-lived, however, for only four days after Harley's resignation, Queen Anne unexpectedly died, and the unprepared Tories went down to ruin. Almost immediately Swift took leave of England, and by the middle of August, 1714, was back in Dublin. Jonathan Swift's career as a Tory journalist, except for such retrospective pieces as he was to write in later years, had ended.

Jonathan Swift as a Tory Pamphleteer

One: Swift's Sense of Audience Prior to 1710 and "The Wickedness of the Age"

I

IN the "Apology" which he added to the fifth edition of *Tale of a Tub* (1710) Swift tells his readers that he had conceived of the work as "a Satyr, that would be useful and diverting." [1] It is interesting to compare this remark with his well-known statement, made in a letter to Pope on September 29, 1725, that "the chief end I propose to my self in all my labors is to vex the world rather than divert it." [2] As the shift in emphasis between these two statements of purpose indicates, in the quarter century which elapsed between the composition of *Tale of a Tub* and *Gulliver's Travels* Swift had experienced a basic change of heart with regard to the nature of his job as a satirist and the ends to which his work might be applied. The man whose epitaph speaks of the *saeva indignatio* which had for so long lacerated his heart and inspired his pen, is a somewhat different person from the young author whose declared intention in his earliest work is to be "useful and diverting." In the process by which Swift, as his career progressed, came increasingly to see his task as a writer in polemical terms and to view his function as one primarily corrective, his experience as a pamphleteer for the Harley–St. John ministry was to play an important and perhaps crucial role. In order to help us better understand this role it will be necessary—before turning to analysis of the tracts themselves—to survey the audiences, the circumstances of appearance, and the general tone and techniques of Swift's major prose works prior to 1710; likewise it will be relevant to discuss Swift's theories of politics and history, especially as they were to influence his views of the profound social and economic changes which were taking place in England during his lifetime. By such a survey we may hope to see more clearly the place Swift's Tory tracts occupy in the context of his early career, and from the perspective thus gained, we will be able to assess the nature of their importance in his development as an artist.

The *Tale of a Tub,* along with its companion pieces—the *Battle of the Books* and the *Mechanical Operation of the Spirit*—has always been recognized as a work somehow standing apart from the body of Swift's writings. Such sustained exuberance seems scarcely in keeping with the gloominess and pessimism which we have come to think of as characteristic ingredients in Swiftian satire. Samuel Johnson found the *Tale* so distinctly different from the rest of Swift's works that he was led privately to question its authorship and publicly to state:

His *Tale of a Tub* has little resemblance to his other pieces. It exhibits vehemence and rapidity of mind, a copiousness of images, and vivacity of diction such as he afterwards never possessed or never exerted. It is of a mode so distinct and peculiar that it must be considered by itself; what is true of that is not true of any thing else which he has written.[3]

There is some evidence that Swift first produced the allegory for the *Tale of a Tub* while still a student at Trinity College.[4] Such an origin, if true, might help account for the work's buoyant quality, for it has about it something of the air of an audacious *jeu d'esprit* designed to display its author's brilliant talents to fullest advantage. Whether or not it was actually begun in college, the bulk of the work in the form we have it today was written while Swift was still in his twenties, and his youth, as he remarks in the "Apology," led him to give "a Liberty to his Pen, which might not suit with maturer Years" (I, 1–2). The pervasively high-spirited tone of the *Tale* is not of a sort which lends itself to easy demonstration in brief quotations; rather it is a quality which the reader senses as an animating force behind the entire work. This is not to say that the *Tale of a Tub* is without highly serious intent or that it is designed to do nothing more than show off its author's wit. Swift displays no lack of moral fervor or indignation in his attack upon the modern corruptions which have infiltrated religion and learning. But although he finds such things appalling, his general manner in the *Tale* tends to focus the reader's attention more upon the amusing absurdity of the follies described than upon the profound threats they pose to society. To the extent that all satire has reform as its ultimate goal, the *Tale* may be said to contain a call to action, but the only immediate response demanded of the reader is a joining in laughter at the expense of the pedants and enthusiasts whose handiwork is anatomized.

The audience toward which the *Tale of a Tub* was directed has been identified for us by Swift in his statement that at the time the work was composed, its author was "a young Gentleman much in the World, and wrote to the Tast [*sic*] of those who were like himself" (I, 1). Equally revealing of Swift's intent are the frequent references throughout the work to the men of wit and taste, the select few, who alone can savor what he has written. Such references, whether seriously intended (as in the "Apology") or ironically (as in the *Tale* itself, when the persona is speaking), help explain something of the special quality of the work. The young Swift, consciously writing for "those who were like himself," seems to have intended his book, at least on a superficial level, as a sort of family joke—the family in question consisting of that comparatively small circle of sophisticates who by education, social background, and personal inclination were capable of fully appreciating the bewildering wealth of esoteric allusion, parody, and digression which Swift offered. To Swift's great misfortune, the ordinary reader of the day missed the point and found the work scandalous. Even so acute a judge as Daniel Defoe, unqualified by education and background to sympathize with Swift's message, dismissed the *Tale* as a mere collection of blasphemies. Churchmen, on the whole, responded similarly, confirming Swift's admission that the book "was not intended for their Perusal" (I, 2).

The relatively straightforward satire of the *Battle of the Books* is of a sort calculated to appeal to an audience wider in scope than that of the *Tale of a Tub*. Though directed at essentially the same group of wits who are addressed in the longer work, the *Battle* contains nothing to outrage the sensibilities of the clergymen, squires, and gentry who would normally rally to support the cause of the Ancients, in what was in many ways a social as well as intellectual battle. Sir William Temple, in a letter of March 30, 1698, had referred to Bentley's attack upon him in the *Dissertation on the Epistles of Phalaris,* and had remarked that he himself had "no mind to Enter the List, with such a Mean, Dull, Unmannerly PEDANT." [5] The disdain expressed here is that of the aristocrat for the boor, and as such it is indicative of the battle lines in the Ancients-Moderns controversy and, by analogy, of Swift's audience. Though the participants in the two controversies were not identical, the dispute between the Ancients and the Moderns, which inspired the *Battle of the Books,* furnished a literary analogy to the economic and political fight between the rising commercial middle class and the older landowning aristocracy. In many ways the Moderns, with their zealous professionalism and their graceless pedantries, were to the supporters of the Ancients as the Dissenter-tradesman class was to the old aristocracy, and the scorn directed at such upstarts was as likely to be aimed at their social origins as at their critical judgments.

For the most part, in the *Battle of the Books* Swift is content, as he had been in the *Tale of a Tub,* to find his opponents more ludicrous than dangerous. The complacency and pretensions of the Moderns are ridiculed, but there is little to suggest that these strutting, puffed-up figures offer any urgent threat to established cultural standards. The section of Parnassus where the Ancients reside, after all, is solid rock, and should the Moderns attack it, we are told, they can only hope to "break their Tools and Hearts; without [inflicting] any Damage . . ." (I, 143). Under the circumstances, laughter is a more appropriate response to their onslaught than is alarm. Furthermore, a certain moderation is introduced into Swift's attack by the ambiguity in his attitude toward the Moderns; for his contempt toward them is far from absolute. In the Parnassus allegory we discover that although the Ancients occupy the top of the mountain, the Moderns do not live in a valley, as we might have expected, but rather on a nearby eminence which is second in height only to the peak itself. Nor are the Ancients (or, at any rate, their proponents) altogether immune from implied criticism, since Swift speaks of the "warm Heads of either Faction" and the "Virulence of both Parties" (I, 142, 143). By such means Swift manages to project the impression of a man who is at least partially above the scene of combat and who looks down with amusement, however unequal, upon both struggling armies.

This air of amused Olympianism is particularly distinct in the *Partridge Papers,* which, though not without serious overtones, are designed more than any of Swift's other sizable satires to elicit pure laughter. That the semiliterate populace should patronize Partridge and his colleagues was a fact that presumably would strike Swift as neither surprising nor particularly amusing; but that men of education and substance should do so, furnished a sufficient cause for civilized laughter. As Bickerstaff remarks (ostensibly in criticism of those who follow Partridge's "false" astrology in preference to his own "legitimate" variety):

. . . I rather wonder, when I observe Gentlemen in the Country, rich enough to serve the Nation in Parliament, poring in *Partrige's* [*sic*] Almanack, to find out the Events of the Year at Home and Abroad; not daring to propose a Hunting-Match, until *Gadbury,* or he, hath fixed the Weather. [II, 142]

But while the contemporary reader was invited to laugh at the egregious charlatanry of Partridge and the gullibility of his patrons, what was perhaps the cream of the jest was reserved for Swift and the small circle of wits who were either in on the joke or clever enough to have detected it from the start. For a final laugh comes at the expense of those readers who, though they might be undeceived by the impostures of astrology, would nevertheless have been duped by their failure to detect Swift's ruse. These were the readers who would have initially responded with a contemptuous dismissal of Bickerstaff's predictions as nothing more than the carping of one ridiculous mountebank at another. For such quarry, Swift sets his trap carefully. Except for a rather suspicious tone of bumptious self-assurance, there is almost nothing in the opening paper, *Predictions for the Year 1708,* to suggest to the casual reader that the forecast is anything other than what it claims to be. The "Person of Quality" who wrote *An Answer to Bickerstaff* (for a time attributed to Swift himself) was one of those who *did* see through the joke, and he expressed his amusement at those who had not by saying, "I very much approve the serious air [Bickerstaff] gives himself in his introduction and conclusion, which hath gone far to give some people of no mean rank an opinion, that the author believes himself" (II, 196). Thus taken in, even many readers who would normally be allies in an attack upon Partridge become fair game for Swift's laughter, and (as the author of the *Answer* points out) they serve as additional gulls for Bickerstaff "and his friends in the secret, [who] laugh often and plentifully in a corner, to reflect how many hundred thousand fools they have already made" (II, 195).

At this early stage in his career it was not only toward literary and social fads that Swift tended to assume a stance of aloof amusement: he was at first inclined to react in much the same way toward the political, and sometimes even the religious squabbles of the day. As we have seen earlier, the young Swift, despite his nominal Whig allegiance, was not deeply involved in political concerns. When, in 1701, Swift made his first appearance as a political controversialist with the *Contests and Dissensions in Athens and Rome,* his performance generated very little heat, offered only the mildest satire, and was in general more a calm and school-teacherish exposition than a fervent polemic. His private letters of the period reflect an air of political detachment or sometimes even nonchalance which is strangely at odds with his later passionate involvement. In a letter on December 16, 1703, to his friend, William Tisdall, for example, he cavalierly remarks concerning the bill against occasional conformity—the issue to which Swift would in 1709 devote a fervent tract: ". . . the very night before the bill went up, a committee of Whig and Tory cats, had a very warm and loud debate upon the roof of our house"; and later in the same letter he comments: "I would be glad to know men's thoughts of it in Ireland: for myself, I am much at a loss, though I was mightily urged by some great people to publish my opinion" (*Correspondence,* I, 39). A few weeks later, on February 3, 1704, again writing to Tisdall, Swift casually dismisses the suggestion that he speak out against "Dissenters and Independents" by remarking, "I would as soon trouble my head to write against a louse or a flea" (*Correspondence,* I, 44).

By 1708, Swift had abandoned much of his earlier insouciance toward politics and had begun to speak his mind, particularly upon such questions as involved the Church and her interests. Of his three major political and religious tracts of this period—*Sentiments of a Church-of-England Man with Respect to Religion and Government* (1708), *Project for the Advancement of Religion and the Reformation of Manners* (1709), and *Argument Against Abolishing Christianity in England* (1708)—two are sober expressions of Swift's growing alarm over the rise of irreligion and faulty principles, and the third is a satiric treatment of the same problem. In these tracts Swift no longer gives the impression (except in parts of the *Argument*) of a wit addressing himself to a select handful of his peers, but rather he directs his message at all nominal supporters of the Church of England. The vices he attacks are not new, and he had, in fact, already dealt with most of them in *Tale of a Tub,* but they have become more than merely laughable for him: he feels now a serious unease over their extending power and its menace to society. Nevertheless, in 1708–9 Swift had not yet reached a sense of crisis, nor was he yet inclined to feel pessimistic about the outcome of the battle developing between the Establishment and its increasingly truculent foes. In the *Sentiments of a Church-of-England Man,* as Ricardo Quintana has said, Swift "chose to lay his views before the reader in a calm, conciliatory manner that seemed to place his whole discussion quite outside the realm of heated controversy." [6] In the course of this statement of his own principles, Swift makes clear his confidence that the fundamentals of religion and government which he advocates are subscribed to by the majority of both Whigs and Tories and opposed by only a minority of extremists in either camp. The over-all effect of even the satirical *Argument Against Abolishing Christianity* is not one of urgency. Regarding the tone of this work, Swift's contemporary and friend, Lord Orrery, remarked: "He judged rightly in imagining that a small treatise, written with a spirit of mirth and freedom, must be more efficacious, than long sermons, or laborious lessons of morality. He endeavours to laugh us into religion; well knowing that we are often laughed out of it." [7]

"I know it is reckoned but a Form of Speech, when Divines complain of the Wickedness of the Age," Swift writes in the *Project for the Advancement of Religion* (1709); "However, I believe, upon a fair Comparison with other Times and Countries, it would be found an undoubted Truth" (II, 45). But that the situation, though serious, is not yet desperate, is indicated by the nature of Swift's suggested solution for the threat posed to society by the forces of faction, irreligion, and fanaticism. In the *Project* he advocates a plan whereby persons who profess to be irreligious or lead "irregular" lives would be denied royal favor and preferment. He suggests that the forms of public piety be rigidly enforced, and that offenders in all walks of life be fined or imprisoned. Swift admits that many laws to similar effects already exist, but he insists upon the need for stricter application of the old laws and maintains that many new laws (such as a midnight curfew for taverns) be passed. If such a regime were instituted in London alone, Swift says, it would

. . . in Time, spread it self over the whole Kingdom. . . . And if Things were once in this Train; that is, if Virtue and Religion were established as the necessary Titles to Reputation and Preferment; and if Vice and Infidelity were not only loaden with Infamy, but made the infallible Ruin of all Mens

Pretensions; our Duty, by becoming our Interest, would take Root in our Natures, and mix with the very Genius of our People; so that it would not be easy for the Example of one wicked Prince, to bring us back to our former Corruptions. [II, 59]

The faith that a few such relatively painless measures could reform society bespeaks a sort of naïve optimism so unlike Swift that some recent commentators have felt obliged to offer the unconvincing suggestion that Swift intended his *Project* to be read ironically. There is no evidence to support such a reading, and there is every reason to believe that Swift, as of 1709, still felt that society needed only to effect a few simple reforms to cure itself of a disease which, though potentially fatal, was as yet not far advanced.

In essence, what Swift urges in the *Project* is that all men, whatever they choose to believe in private, should be required to show in public at least a pretense of respect for religion. Admittedly, such a system would tend to increase hypocrisy, but Swift maintains that piety, even when it is only assumed, is much to be preferred to open ridicule of the Church. In expressing this opinion, Swift is taking a stand upon a question which was beginning to be much debated at this period—namely, to what degree, if at all, was it permissible to subject the mysteries of religion to bantering comment. That this topic should be of particular interest to Swift, who had himself been widely accused of blasphemy after the *Tale of a Tub,* was only natural, especially since its ramifications had a serious bearing upon his concept of the audience for whom he wrote and the effects he hoped to produce.

In 1708, the year before the *Project* was written, the Earl of Shaftesbury had published his *Letter Concerning Enthusiasm,* in which he contended that the ability to survive prolonged laughter is a sign by which true ideas and institutions can be distinguished from false. He proposed, therefore, that ridicule (which he insisted should always be urbane and good-humored) be more freely applied in society, with a view toward the exposure of fanaticism and error. Shaftesbury's suggestion was immediately attacked by those who felt that an inevitable result of endorsing ridicule as a criterion for establishing truth, would be the encouragement of public expressions of contempt for the nation's most revered beliefs, in particular, those of revealed religion. In response to this attack, Shaftesbury averred his own complete faith in the verities of Christianity, but he continued to maintain, as in his essay on *The Freedom of Wit and Humour,* that "a freedom of raillery, a liberty in decent language to question everything, and an allowance of unravelling or refuting any argument, without offence to the arguer" [8] could serve as a means toward socially desirable ends.[9]

On the first appearance of the *Letter Concerning Enthusiasm,* its authorship had been ascribed by some to Swift. Writing on September 14, 1708, to Ambrose Philips, Swift remarks:

Here has been an Essay of Enthusiasm lately publisht that has run mightily, and is very well writt, All my Friends will have me to be the Author, sed ego non credulus illis [Virgil, *Eclogues,* IX, 34]. By the free Whiggish thinking I should rather take it to be yours: But mine it is not. [*Correspondence,* I, 100]

That Swift should be considered a likely author for the *Letter Concerning Enthusiasm* is not surprising, since he was notorious for having only a few years earlier applied satire and ridicule toward the subject of religion. But by 1708 Swift had had occasion to consider the consequences of laughter at the expense of religion, and in that same year (in the *Argument Against Abolishing Christianity*) he posed the ironic question:

If Christianity were once abolished, how would the Free-Thinkers, the strong Reasoners, and the Men of profound Learning be able to find another Subject so calculated in all Points whereon to display their Abilities [?] What wonderful Productions of Wit should we be deprived of, from those whose Genius, by continual Practice hath been wholly turned upon Raillery and Invectives against Religion; and [who] would therefore never be able to shine or distinguish themselves upon any other Subject. [II, 36]

Swift presumably felt a more than ordinary impulse to take a clear stand on this question. He had doubtless been appalled four years earlier to find the *Tale of a Tub* seized by "Free-Thinkers" as a club with which to beat the Church, and he would now naturally have been glad of an opportunity to disassociate himself from such unwanted allies. Swift, of course, continued to insist that the *Tale* itself, far from being an attack upon religion, was in reality a work which ridiculed only "the Follies of Fanaticism and Superstition," while celebrating "the Church of *England* as the most perfect of all others in Discipline and Doctrine" (I, 2). Yet, he could not deny to himself that the work had been almost uniformly ill-received among the pious and that many had classified its author as precisely the sort of coffee-house wit who amused himself and his fellows by making light of religious belief. So disconcerting a public response—one reflecting the wide discrepancy between the author's own ideas and those of his readers concerning the essential nature of the work—is indicative of the degree to which Swift had failed to clarify in his own mind the audience for which he intended his *Tale of a Tub*.

As I have mentioned earlier, the *Tale,* though sufficiently serious in its implications, has about it something of the air of a private joke composed for its author's own amusement. As such, it is particularly susceptible to misinterpretation by those who, operating outside the author's personal frame of moral reference, are apt to overlook or misread the signposts he has provided. When to such difficulties is added the fact that the *Tale* is a sustained piece of irony consistently requiring simultaneous comprehension on two or more levels, it is scarcely surprising that so many of Swift's contemporaries were misled. For coffee-house wits it was easy to read the satire on modern learning in the *Tale of a Tub* as a general attack on pedantry. Since no one was more apt to be heavily pedantic than authors of religious and theological tomes, and since many of Swift's targets (such as Richard Bentley and William Wotton) were pious and orthodox Church of England men as well as modernists, it seemed natural to some to consider the *Tale* as a sly dig at religious self-delusion.

Nor would the fable necessarily alter such a conclusion. A totally unsophisticated reader approaching the history of Peter, Jack, and Martin would see nothing more than a simple story; while at the other end of the scale, an ideally knowing reader would presumably understand not only all the nuances of the allegory, but would also appreciate its basic expression of Church of England orthodoxy. Unfortunately, Swift's book encountered the great mass of readers between these two extremes, and a considerable number, perhaps even a majority, saw only a frivolous treatment of religious history to which they responded either with horror or amusement—in either case for reasons quite different from those Swift had intended. In effect, the *Tale* merely experienced in its own era the sort of fate that most literary works come to suffer with the passage of time, when to a greater or lesser degree each succeeding generation imposes its own new reading upon the works it has received from the past. I do not mean to suggest that no one aside from Swift and a handful of his friends was capable of understanding the *Tale of a Tub,* but only that the widespread misinterpretation which greeted the work—a misinterpretation so disastrous in terms of Swift's career in the Church—was at least partially ascribable to its young author's lack of a clearly formulated concept of audience.

As we have seen, however, by 1708 Swift had begun to issue unequivocal statements designed to disassociate himself from the sort of wits who had so relished the "blasphemy" of the *Tale of a Tub.* In addition to the works already cited, he composed in that year the *Remarks Upon a Book Intitled, "The Rights of the Christian Church,"* in which the target for his anger was the Deist, Matthew Tindal, who had satirized clerical pedantry in the course of an attack upon state-supported religion. Significantly, among those who joined with Swift in denouncing Tindal's laughter at the expense of religious writers was William Wotton, a man who in all likelihood would have expected the author of the *Tale of a Tub* to be Tindal's natural ally and sympathizer. Swift's reply to Tindal's criticism, like Wotton's own answer, was to point out that although "Free-Thinkers" might sneer at "Pedantry, and Cant, . . . and insignificant Terms in the Writings of the Clergy" (II, 81), such things as dullness and obscurity were offenses far less serious than the *new* pedantries of irreligion and fashionable skepticism. The way in which "the Fear of being thought Pedants hath been of pernicious Consequence" (IX, 67) was to become a recurrent theme in Swift's later writings—particularly those dealing with style, such as: *Tatler* 230 (1710), *Hints Towards an Essay on Conversation* (*ca.* 1710), the *Proposal for Correcting the English Tongue* (1712), and *Letter to a Young Clergyman* (1720).

In the foregoing brief survey of Swift's writings prior to 1710 I have sought to demonstrate two related points: (1) that in his early works Swift frequently seemed to write with no clear general audience in mind and that, accordingly, his works sometimes give the impression of having been composed less for publication than for circulation among his own circle of acquaintances; and (2) that although Swift was obviously concerned from the first with the dangers to society from enthusiasm and the resultant corruptions in religion and learning, the attitudes and remedies promulgated in his early writings indicate that he viewed these dangers as neither urgent nor so far advanced as to be beyond relatively easy control. By 1708, the reception accorded the *Tale of a Tub* had obliged Swift to reconsider the nature of his intended audience and the sorts of moral ends toward which his work might be applied. It is my contention that it was during the course of Swift's career as a Tory pamphleteer and immediately after that these questions were largely resolved—a resolution which was inspired by Swift's sharply increased sense of the seriousness of the danger to society from those forces he had earlier found more laughable than urgently threatening.

II

Swift was in no sense an original thinker on history, and his views on the subject were those common and traditional among conservatives in Augustan England. In no one place does he offer an organized formulation of his opinions, yet almost all his major works reflect, either by implication or by precept, his adherence to the cyclical theory of history. This theory, which in its basic form extends back to Polybius, postulates that man's fundamental nature is at all times and everywhere essentially the same. It does not follow, however, that all societies are the same or that civilization will remain at a constant level; for men are subject to the influences of environment (especially those of climate and luxury), and these will stimulate different humors and inspire varying behavior. Since conditions differ widely from era to era as well as from place to place, the course of history will in general be cyclical. Civilizations will rise, flourish, decay, and be replaced, but culture is not cumulative, and hence there can be no steady social progress. Furthermore, when cultural ascendancy is relinquished by one people, circumstances may be such that there are no others capable of assuming the succession.

In this latter point the cyclical theory of history, as promulgated in the seventeenth and early eighteenth centuries, gave rise to the nagging fear that culture might vanish altogether from the world, perhaps never to be revived, except on the chance that suitable conditions would eventually reappear. More immediately pressing, however, was the fear that one's own country might at any time lose its temporary ascendancy and be plunged back into barbarism. Dark ages of varying length and geographic range have existed throughout history, and their recurrence, as predicated by the cyclical theory, posed a constant threat. As Swift wrote on January 6, 1709, in answer to Archbishop King's expression of optimism over the future prospects of religion:

. . . the World is divided into two Sects, those that hope the best, and those that fear the worst; your Grace is of the former, which is the wiser, the nobler, and most pious Principle; and although I endeavour to avoid being of the other, yet upon this Article [i.e., the fate of religious belief] I have sometimes strange Weaknesses. I compare true Religion to Learning and Civility which have ever been in the World, but very often shifted their Scenes; sometimes entirely leaving whole Countries where they have long flourished . . . ; how far the wickedness of a Nation may provoke God Almighty to inflict so great a Judgement, is terrible to think. [*Correspondence*, I, 117]

The cyclical theory, while it precluded any hope of step-by-step progress toward ultimate perfection, did not in its essential form stipulate an inevitable descending spiral of history. To many Christians in the seventeenth and eighteenth centuries, however, the gradual decline of human society was a theologically demonstrable fact, and as such, it came to be incorporated as a part of the cyclical theory. Some men might cherish visions of a potential earthly paradise, but to Swift and countless of his fellow clergymen, the lessons of the Bible seemed clear: original sin, which had brought about man's expulsion from Eden and had left him innately corrupt, had inevitably produced a general tendency in mankind toward degeneration, and this process, barring some unexpected act of divine intervention, would continue until finally halted by the day of wrath. Naturally, the rate of decline need not always and everywhere be the same—no nation or age would be entirely without its noble and virtuous men, and it was possible that in certain times and places the processes of degeneration might be arrested or even temporarily reversed. However, when history was viewed in larger terms, the over-all progression was inexorably downward. The course of history, in a favored analogy, could be likened to the life of a single man. As he advanced through life, a man might experience alternate periods of sickness and health; any one of his diseases might be controlled by medicine or perhaps even cured entirely; yet, whatever small victories he might win over decay, in the long run a man's progress, like society's, was predictably in the direction of increasing sickness and decline.[10]

Though themes of social decline and degeneracy had been important ingredients in Swift's works from the start of his career as an author, we have seen how little there is in his writings prior to 1710 to match the insistent note of imminent crisis which so strongly characterizes the bulk of his later work. Concerning the differences between Swift's 1710–14 productions and his earlier works, Herbert Davis remarks: "He is writing [in his Tory tracts] no longer as a wit, a young gentleman much in the world, showing off his skill as he makes fun of the world of religion and learning; he is now using his pen to get certain things done." [11] As the next chapter will demonstrate, the enormous success of Swift's tracts in getting "things done" is at least partially based upon a far greater attention to audience and its requirements than he had hitherto been inclined to pay. But spectacular as the public success of his tracts was, it would seem that the greatest job of persuasion Swift performed in these years was upon himself. For the man who, outside his religious concerns, had formerly evidenced little more than tepid interest and polite amusement at politics, was now transformed into the party stalwart who for the next four years steadily maintained that the nation's prosperity, and indeed, its very survival depended upon a continuance of Tory rule. The *Journal to Stella,* his private letters of this period, and his whole subsequent career furnish evidence to indicate that what Swift experienced during his service for the Harley–St. John ministry aroused in him a feeling that the nation was in desperate circumstances from which only Tories could save it.

The process by which Swift came to feel that society was in imminent peril did not involve a fundamental change of heart or philosophy. If prior to 1710 Swift was on the whole more amused than terrified by the follies and corruptions of modern life, it was not because he was oblivious to their dangers, but merely that those dangers seemed less than overwhelming. The sense of gloom and alarm in Swift's later works is not so much absent in his pre-1710 writings as it is muted and to some extent overshadowed by the laughter. Yet, though Swift had always been aware of the threat, his recognition of its dimensions and immediacy became immensely heightened after 1710, in much the same way that his friend Pope's pessimistic view of cultural decline—already implicit in the prophecy of Dulness in the *Dunciad* of 1728—was to become acute and dominant with the fulfillment of that prophecy in the *Dunciad* of 1742.

Swift's increased sense of the situation's urgency, developed during four years as a Tory pamphleteer and heralding a new tone in his ensuing works, marks a significant stage in his career. Identifying himself, as he had never been able to before, with the shapers of the country's destiny, Swift abandoned his earlier pose of dilettante unconcern with the grubby realities of politics. As he found himself perforce immersed in the battle, he became convinced that the whole complex of his old enemies—the Deists, the Dissenters, the Grub Street hacks, and all the infinitely presumptuous corrupters of religion and learning—had become too dangerous to laugh away; they had grown in insolence and power to the point where, unless vigorously checked, they could carry out what Swift saw as their all but avowed intention to destroy society.

I do not mean to suggest, of course, that this process was either sudden or dramatic. Swift's new sense of urgency was, after all, only a natural extension of the direction in which his thought had already been tending—given Swift's outlook, the drift of the times was one which inevitably would have produced in him a serious alarm over society's health. Yet, when all reservations have been made, there does remain a certain element of shocked discovery in Swift's 1710 reaction. From his new vantage point *inside* the government, Swift was in a better position than he had ever been before for observing and cataloguing those disruptive forces which, when he had viewed them from the outside, had always seemed contemptible rather than frightening. His response, as reflected in the Tory tracts, was a depth of party feeling which was in many ways more pronounced than Harley's. It is ironic to read in the *Journal to Stella* how Swift, within months after Harley had recruited him to the cause, begins to chafe at the treasurer's annoying air of complacency and his slowness in ousting the "Whig Dogs" from office. To Swift, once his sense of alarm had been aroused, Harley's procrastination and composure in the face of Whig provocations seemed inexplicable. The whole modern idea that there might be two or more political parties of equal legitimacy was one which Harley, as a practicing politician, understood in a way that Swift never did. In Swift's view, men might legitimately disagree on particulars or policies, but since there could only be one basic truth, disagreement on fundamental principle meant that somebody was simply wrong. It followed that at least one of any two given parties was a "Faction" and, thus, ultimately treasonous. It is on this basis that Swift's

sometimes excessive party zeal becomes understandable. However mixed
and ambiguous may have been the motives that initially led him to lend
his services to the Harley–St. John ministry, the Swift who addresses his
readers in the Tory tracts is a man who never doubts that he is fighting in
the desperate cause of national survival.

Two: The Audience of Swift's Tory Tracts

ＩF, as Aristotle puts it, the art of rhetoric lies in "discovering in the particular case what are the available means of persuasion,"[1] then it follows that the more specific an audience the rhetor has in mind, the more easily he will be able to choose those arguments most likely to persuade. In attempting to ascertain the audience toward which Jonathan Swift directed his political tracts, we must turn to the works themselves for our primary evidence, although outside sources may furnish valuable clues. It is from Swift's references to his audience and, more importantly, from the tone and nature of his arguments, that we may best surmise the groups of readers he hoped to reach; for if it is the nature of the audience which determines what appeals are to be used, we may by reverse process examine the nature of the appeals for clues as to the intended audience.

A large proportion of Swift's publications as a Tory pamphleteer consists of a multitude of brief tracts more in the nature of timely broadsheets than extended political controversy. Of this kind are such works as the *Short Character of His Excellency Thomas Earl of Wharton* (1710), *Some Advice to the October Club* (1712), *Letter to a Whig Lord* (1712), *Publick Spirit of the Whigs* (1714), and numerous others. In this category too may be placed Swift's *Examiner* papers (1710–11), which, though written as a series and possessing some elements of general unity, are primarily brief independent essays. Opposed to such brief tracts are the book-length works whose scope offers an opportunity for extended argument, i.e., *Conduct of the Allies* (1711) and *History of the Four Last Years of the Queen* (1713).

To speak dogmatically of a single "audience" for so wide a range of works written over a period of four years naturally would be misleading.

Swift's primary audience may vary from pamphlet to pamphlet or from section to section of any one tract, and in addition, one or more perceptible secondary audiences may be addressed. However, it remains possible after a careful reading of Swift's political tracts to determine within general limits the particular social and economic group toward which he made his most consistent primary appeal. In attempting to ascertain the identity of this group we must rely upon four kinds of evidence. First, there are the explicit statements of Swift himself. Here and there in his political tracts Swift, either by direct statement or by reference, indicates who he imagined his readers to be. Second, there is much important evidence to be gathered from the tone and character of his appeals—both by the emotions he seeks to exploit and by the nature of what he attacks, we may obtain a clearer picture of those he wishes to reach. Third, and less directly, there is the testimony furnished by our knowledge of the political and social structure of early eighteenth-century England. Fourth and last, there are such clues as exist in contemporary references to the pamphlets and their effect. On the basis of these criteria, and without in any way precluding a wide variety of secondary audiences, we may say that the primary audience Jonathan Swift hoped to reach through his pamphlets in defense of the Tory ministry—the group to which he most consistently made his appeals—was one composed of the smaller English country squires and the clergymen, freeholders, and tenants who made up the social complex dominated by such squires.

There are, of course, such exceptions as occur primarily in the briefer tracts where Swift may take occasion to appeal to restricted groups he elsewhere addresses only peripherally. *Some Advice to the October Club* and *Letter to a Whig Lord* are examples of tracts in which Swift, as his titles indicate, directs his arguments toward specific limited groups—in one case the High-Flier Tory extremists thirsting for more Whig blood and in the other the lukewarm Whigs, who, like Swift himself in 1710, seemed likely prospects for conversion. In both cases Swift's tone and approach are at variance with his usual practice elsewhere in his political writings. Normally aggressively contemptuous of Whig and Tory "extremists" alike, Swift is respectful and in general anxious to avoid offense as he defends the Harley–St. John ministry before the "true Lovers of our Constitution in Church and State" [2] who made up the Jacobite sympathizers of the October Club. Likewise, there is an altogether uncustomary note of nonpartisanship in Swift's *Letter to a Whig Lord,* wherein the author, who elsewhere so consistently characterizes the Whigs as the party of open disloyalty and irreligion, now temperately remarks: "The Dispute between your Lordship and Me, hath, I think, no manner of Relation to what, in the common Style of these Times, are called *Principles;* wherein both Parties seem well enough to agree, if we will but allow their Professions" (VI, 123).

Neither the extremist Tories addressed in the first of these pamphlets nor the moderate Whigs appealed to in the second are normally central targets in Swift's pamphlets. This is not to deny that there is much in the bulk of Swift's political tracts that would have pleased the October Club's members and much else that might conceivably have persuaded luke-warm Whigs to reconsider their political allegiances, but in his two major political works, *Conduct of the Allies* and *History of the Four Last Years of the Queen,* as well as in most of his briefer tracts, Swift addresses himself to the October Club Tories only by implication and to the moderate Whigs scarcely at all. Had he been seriously interested in winning Whig converts, Swift would have been far less inclined to stress the irredeemable wickedness of the Whig party. It is true that Swift occasionally, as in *Examiner* 18, proclaims his desire

. . . to undeceive those well-meaning People, who have been drawn unaware into a wrong Sense of Things, either by the common Prejudices of Education and Company, the great personal Qualities of some Party-leaders, or the foul Misrepresentations that were constantly made of all who durst differ from [the Whig ministry] in the smallest Article. [III, 31]

But that Swift does not consider the Whigs as belonging among the innocently misled is indicated by the whole tenor of his attack, for the faults Swift habitually ascribes to them are not of a sort that can be dismissed as the results of ignorance or lack of judgment. As atheists, traitors, and misers, the Whigs are beyond redemption, and Swift seems to have felt that most Whig sympathizers who were amenable to conversion had, like himself, already completed the process. In *Examiner* 43, after a bitter attack on Whig policies, he remarks: "I do not include within [the Whigs], any of those, who have been misled by Ignorance, or seduced by plausible Pretences . . . : Because, I believe, the greatest Part of such well-meaning People, are now thoroughly converted" (III, 165).

In *Advice to the October Club* and *Letter to a Whig Lord* the primary audience has conveniently been identified for us, but it would be naïve to accept at face value in every case Swift's own statements as to his intended readers. In *Examiner* 36, for example, we are told, "I write this Paper for the Sake of the *Dissenters*" (III, 126). But what follows is an aggressive attack in which Dissenters, who are characterized as king-killers and fanatics, are ominously warned to disperse themselves and cease making trouble, lest right-thinking men be obliged to withdraw their grudging toleration. From the tone and nature of Swift's arguments, it is apparent that this *Examiner* was intended for the edification of High Church readers, who would enjoy seeing the nonconformists scarified, rather than for the ostensibly addressed Dissenters, who could only be angered and appalled by it. Yet despite the occasional disingenuousness of Swift's references to his intended audience, it is from such references scattered throughout his political tracts that we may begin to discern the identity of those for whom he wrote and whose opinions he hoped to influence. Disregarding as too general (though not necessarily insincere) Swift's random assertions that he wrote merely for all patriots and men of reason, we find that such references as Swift makes to his intended readers indicate that he had a more distinct and specific group in mind.

References to rural and provincial readers—those far removed from London where the political drama is enacted and political news originates—are frequent in Swift's tracts. Typical of such references are his remarks in the *History of the Four Last Years of the Queen:*

Discourses upon Subjects relating to the Publick usually seem to be calculated only for *London,* and some few Miles about it; while the Authors suppose their Readers to be informed of several Particulars, to which, those who live remote, are for the Generality utter Strangers. Most People, who frequent this Town, acquire a sort of Smattering (such as it is) which qualifies them for reading a Pamphlet, and finding out what is meant by Innuendo's or Hints at Facts or Persons, or initial Letters of Names; wherein Gentlemen at distance, although perhaps of much better Understandings, are wholly in the dark. [VII, 2]

Recurring throughout the political tracts are such indications that Swift consciously directed his major efforts toward a provincial audience rather than one composed of the political sophisticates of London. In the *Examiner* numbers 26 ("At least, all I can pretend, is to undeceive the

Ignorant, and those at Distance" [III, 76]) and 32 ("I shall take Occasion to hint at some Particularities . . . for the Sake of those at distance, or who may not be thoroughly informed" [III, 109]); in the *Conduct of the Allies* ("It is the Folly of too many, to mistake the Eccho of a *London* Coffee-house for the Voice of the Kingdom" [VI, 53]); in the *History of the Four Last Years of the Queen* ("I am persuaded that . . . those at Home, who live too remote from the Scene of Business to be rightly informed, will not be displeased with this Account . . ." [VII, 75]); and in many similar references scattered throughout the political tracts, Swift's concern with the rural reader becomes apparent. In an age of poor and slow communications, the sources of political information available to the reader who lived away from London were necessarily few, and he was apt to be starved for news. Swift was aware of this situation, and satisfying the provincial reader's appetite with such news and information as was favorable to the Tory ministry was one of the primary goals he set himself.

A subsidiary audience which Swift occasionally refers to is "posterity." By implication, most of Swift's tracts are at least obliquely addressed to the readers of the future, and in the briefer works (as in *Examiner* 18) he sometimes bemoans the fact that much of what he writes will inevitably one day be too obscure for posterity to understand. It is in the longer works, however, and particularly in the *History of the Four Last Years of the Queen,* that he most explicitly assumes the role of historian. In his preface to that work he remarks:

Therefore, as I pretend to write with the utmost impartiality, the following History of the four last years of her Majesty's reign, in order to undeceive prejudiced persons at present, as well as posterity; I am persuaded in my own mind, as likewise by the advice of my oldest and wisest friends, that I am doing my duty to God and man by endeavouring to set future ages right in their judgment of that happy reign; and, as a faithful historian, I cannot suffer falsehoods to run on any longer. . . . [VII, xxxiv]

Swift's role and function as a historian writing his political tracts for the benefit of future generations will be discussed elsewhere in this study. It may suffice here to point out that the members of posterity Swift envisages as forming part of his intended audience are in much the same position as were Swift's contemporaries who lived away from London. A distance in time even more than a distance in space is apt to shroud political events in a haze of missed allusions and unappreciated nuances. In either case, Swift sees as part of his function the duty of informing those who might otherwise remain ignorant of the truth. Thus, though posterity forms an important portion of Swift's intended readership, he does not feel obliged to appeal to it in special terms. Throughout his appeal to posterity Swift makes the tacit assumption that his future readers will share his own basic regard for such things as the Church of England and the royal prerogative. Thus, for practical purposes, Swift deals with his readers of the future much as if they were contemporaries who, like the provincial readers who form his major audience, merely happen to be removed from the center of events.

Confirming Swift's claim that he writes for readers outside London are the general tone and nature of his appeals, and in examining these we may determine more precisely which sections of the rural population he chose as his targets. There are two opposing sets of terms that run through Swift's political tracts like a leitmotif. On the one hand there is the "Landed-Interest," by which Swift means not only those who own land as the traditional source of their income but also those who share a general identity of interest with the property-holding class—the rural clergy, the yeoman freeholders, and the tenant farmers. Opposed to the "Landed Men" is the group Swift characterizes by such terms as the "Monied-Interest," the "Stock-Jobbers," and various similar epithets. Allied with this group are not only the men of commercial wealth, but a wide fringe of hangers-on composed of Dissenters and the urban working classes. Over and over again in Swift's tracts this set of opponents is pictured as struggling for political control of England, and it is primarily in terms of these two contending forces, rather than in terms of Whigs versus Tories, that Swift views the political arena.

From the beginning of his career as a Tory pamphleteer Swift made clear how he felt about the new men of wealth who were making their power felt in the political world. In *Examiner* 14, the second he wrote, he remarks: "We have seen a great Part of the Nation's Money got into the Hands of those, who by their Birth, Education and Merit, could pretend no higher than to wear our Liveries" (III, 12). The use of "our" is significant, for it not only reflects Swift's own sense of identification with the landed gentry, but his assumption of such an identification on his readers' part. In *Examiner* 21, he characterizes the men of mercantile fortune as those who "come with the Spirit of *Shop-keepers* to frame Rules for the Administration of Kingdoms; or, as if they thought the whole Art of Government consisted in the Importation of *Nutmegs,* and the Curing of *Herrings*" (III, 48). Such denunciations of the "Mon-ied-Interest" are frequent, and the tone of the attack becomes particularly strong in Swift's two longer tracts. In the first sentence of the preface to the *Conduct of the Allies* Swift charges the Whigs with "openly profess-ing a separate Interest from the Bulk of the Landed Men . . ." (VI, 5), and later on we are told how

. . . a Set of Upstarts, who had little or no part in the *Revolution* [of 1688], but valued themselves by their Noise and pretended Zeal when the Work was over, were got into Credit at Court, by the Merit of becoming Undertakers and Projectors of Loans and Funds: These, finding that the Gentlemen of Estates were not willing to come into their Measures, fell upon those new Schemes of raising Mony, in order to create a Mony'd-Interest, that might in time vie with the Landed, and of which they hoped to be at the Head. [VI, 10]

It is such men, we are repeatedly told, who wish to prolong the war in order "to enrich Usurers and Stock-jobbers; and to cultivate the perni-cious Designs of a Faction, by destroying the Landed-Interest" (VI, 59). One could cite many similar passages from the *History of the Four Last Years of the Queen* and the shorter tracts as well. Swift's attitude is uncompromising, and he always assumes in such cases that his readers will share his scorn for the men of commercial wealth. Appropriately, among the most frequent of the private vices he ascribes to Whig leaders, in particular the Duke of Marlborough, is avarice—in Swift's eyes an inevitable concomitant of the mercantile spirit.

The sharpness of Swift's animus against the "Monied-Interest" and his assumption of a similar feeling among his provincial readers can be best understood in relationship to the gradual social revolution that had been taking place in England since Cromwell's time. Ever since the Middle Ages political power had been largely divided between the monarch, the hereditary aristocracy, and what was sometimes loosely referred to as the "Country Party." The backbone of this latter classification consisted of the rural, estate-owning gentry. In the days of Queen Anne, as in previous centuries, the overwhelming majority of the House of Commons was elected from rural constituencies, and the country squires were in most cases able to control both the choice and election of candidates. Since 1430 the vote had been given to forty shilling freeholders. Primarily intended were those who received an annual income of forty shillings or more from land, but since the law spoke only of "property," the definition was often stretched to include mortgages, leaseholds, and similar holdings. The yeoman freeholder who owned his small farm could normally be depended upon to accept the political influence of the local squire. As Robert Walcott puts it:

Theoretically the freeholder could make an independent choice, but in practice this freedom was limited to choosing between candidates previously fixed upon at informal meetings of the local landowners. Moreover, the freeholder was often a tenant for some other land and amenable to pressure from the landlord.[3]

Such pressure was customarily applied.

Writing of electioneering in mid-eighteenth-century England, Sir Lewis Namier remarks: "The regular formula for candidates in the counties was to ask the 'Gentlemen, Clergy, and Freeholders' for their votes and interest—'interest' denoting the influence which they could bring to bear on dependants."[4] Freeholders who chose to vote against the candidate endorsed by the estate owners ran considerable risks. Aside from such personal pressures as a large landowner might bring to bear upon men who were partially dependent upon him, the squire was more often than not the local magistrate and justice of the peace. Since voting was not private and was recorded in open poll books, it was a rare freeholder who exercised political independence. Like the freeholders, the clergy could generally be relied upon to vote with the "Landed-Interest." Some clergymen were landowners themselves, and many more depended upon the country squires for their benefices. Politically and economically they held an identity of interest with the members of the landowning class, who likewise, in matters of religion, were traditionally staunch supporters of the Church of England.

The country squire of late seventeenth- and early eighteenth-century England might be a man of considerable wealth and estate, but more often he was a man of modest fortune, sometimes barely a few steps

beyond the yeoman freeholder in wealth—his social and political dominance being based primarily upon his standing as a gentleman rather than
upon his economic status. Toward the end of the seventeenth century,
however, the members of the smaller rural gentry experienced a serious
threat to their political power as, in the years following the Civil War,
there was a tendency for estates to grow in size. Through marriages and
purchases, aristocratic families started accumulating massive estates, and
the smaller squires found themselves increasingly dwarfed by the baronial
hugeness of their neighbors' holdings. At the same time, the new men of
wealth, whose fortunes had been amassed in the period of commercial
expansion which followed the Civil War, were likewise busy in the
accumulation of estates—the time-honored first step toward acquiring
gentility. Writing of the situation at the beginning of the eighteenth
century, Dorothy Marshall says:

It was his relationship to the land that gave a man his obvious and unchal-
lenged place in the social hierarchy, for, though no longer the sole key to
wealth, it was still its most unmistakable symbol and the channel through
which political power flowed. . . . Because land was everywhere recognized
as being the basis of social and political power it was eagerly coveted. . . .
[T]here were no restrictions on its transfer between class and class, so that
the first aim of the financial upstart was to purchase an estate.[5]

It had, of course, long been the custom for the wealthy middle-class
merchant to invest his money in land and set himself up as a country
gentleman, but in Swift's day such men who bought land did so more and
more for its symbolic value—their real wealth continued to derive from
investments and capital, and hence their basic interests frequently remained different from or even hostile to those of the older "Landed Men."
Likewise, in many of the older aristocratic families with massive country
estates, income from sources other than land came to play a large or even
dominant role in dictating political interests. In these circumstances it was
only natural that the smaller squires should resent the forces which were
deposing them from power, and that such resentment should focus upon
the "Monied-Interest." Regarding this state of affairs, J. H. Plumb comments:

As the social and political power of the magnates grew, that of the lesser
gentry diminished. Those who had once been courted were now ignored.

Naturally, they began to look back to a world of the past in which they believed they had possessed undisputed control of their countryside. So men whose fathers had voted for Shaftesbury or welcomed William III as a deliverer turned Tory. What strength and vigour the Tory party possessed in the early part of the century sprang from the social animosity of the country gentlemen of modest means. . . .[6]

Thus, it is among an audience of lesser rural gentry, clergymen, and freeholders that Swift's vigorously expressed concern over the growing political power of the mercantile classes would find its readiest response. Many a country squire must have imagined he saw his own situation in Swift's description of how during the war the new men of wealth through mortgages and loans had so far dispossessed the smaller rural landowners that

. . . the Gentlemen of Estates were in effect but Tenants to these New Landlords; many of whom were able in time to force the Election of Burroughs out of the Hands of those who had been the old Proprietors and Inhabitants. This was arrived to such a Height, that a very few Years more of War and Funds would have clearly cast the Balance on the Money'd Side. [VII, 70]

At the time Swift wrote his political tracts, the country squires, despite the growing encroachments of the "Stock-Jobbers," still retained the greater part of their political power, and without their support no party could hope to rule for long. The bulk of the smaller rural gentry was by tradition royalist and Tory in sympathy, and Swift, by constantly identifying the Whigs with the despised Dissenters, Republicans, and, above all, the "Monied-Interest," sought to bolster that sympathy. Such bolstering was deemed necessary because among the antipathies of the country squire perhaps none were greater than his hatred of Papists. In the War of the Spanish Succession, as in the War of the League of Augsburg, it was the threat posed to England's Protestant succession that more than anything else had roused the kingdom to unity. While Swift labeled the Whigs king-killers, schismatics, and shopkeepers, his Whig counterparts just as insistently confronted the Tories with the damaging and plausible charge of Jacobitism. Whatever natural sympathy the country squires might feel toward the Tory party, as long as the Pretender lay across the Channel waiting his chance, their support could not be taken for granted.

They had to be convinced that their patriotic and religious, as well as their personal, interests would be best served by a Tory ministry, and it was this job of convincing that Swift set out to do in his political pamphlets.

In addition to what has already been cited to indicate that Swift's primary audience was composed of the lesser rural gentry and such voters as they dominated, there is contemporary evidence to show that it was in this class that the pamphlets were most widely distributed. In *Examiner* 28 Swift begins a letter supposedly written by a Tory member of Parliament with the statement: "I am a *Country Member,* and constantly send a Dozen of your Papers down to my Electors" (III, 89). Nor was the practice of this *"Country Member"* an isolated one. Referring to the *Conduct of the Allies,* Swift tells Stella:

I dined in the city, and was with the printer, who has now a fifth edition of the *Conduct,* &c. it is in small, and sold for six-pence; they have printed as many as three editions, because they are to be sent in numbers into the country by great men, &c. who subscribe for hundreds.[7]

The Whigs were well aware of the pains that were taken to distribute Swift's tracts among the rural districts and were resentful. The Whig author who replied to Swift's *Remarks on the Barrier Treaty* with a pamphlet entitled *Remarks upon Remarks,* bitterly comments:

And his Party find Money somewhere or other to buy his Libels by Dozens, and Disperse them about the Country to Poyson the Minds of the People too easily impos'd upon by the plausible Pretence of a Concern for the Public Interest. I have been told they have bundled 'em up with *Briefs* and Fast-Prayers, and distributed 'em by *Apparators* gratis to the poorer Vicars and Curates.[8]

As the last quotation indicates, it was frequently the local clergy, with their access to both gentry and freeholders, who disseminated the arguments Swift furnished. J. Durden, writing to Harley from Scarborough on December 5, 1710, remarks (after denouncing the inroads of the Whig *Observator* and the *Review*):

The honest parson before mentioned [a Mr. Docker] takes abundance of pains to apply the remedy where it is wanted. Mr. Hungerford [the Tory member for Scarborough] sends him the "Examiner" down every Thursday: it comes hither on Sunday and after evening service the parson usually invites a good number of his friends to his house, where he first reads over the paper, and then comments upon the text; and all the week after carries it about with him to read to such of his parishioners as are weak in the faith, and have not yet the eyes of their understanding opened; so that it is not doubted but that he will in time make as many converts to the true interest of the State, as ever he did to the Church.[9]

Likewise, the audience, the purpose, and the effectiveness of Swift's pamphlets are all indicated by Dr. William Stratford, a don at Christ Church, Oxford, when on December 4, 1711, he writes to Harley regarding the *Conduct of the Allies*: "The book of the management of the allies and the late ministry &c. takes, as much as you could wish it. It will put the country gentlemen in the temper you desire, they are very ready to battle it at home for a peace abroad." [10]

Thus, we may say that, although the audience to which Swift addresses himself in his political pamphlets may vary from tract to tract or from place to place within any given work, it is nevertheless possible to discern the identity of the class toward which he most consistently directs his appeals, particularly in his more sizable works. As a "historian" setting the record straight, Swift addresses himself to posterity; as a patriot concerned with his country's welfare, he addresses himself to all reasonable and honest men; but as a practical and accomplished propagandist, he addresses himself most directly to an audience much more immediate and specific than either of these. From the evidence furnished by his direct references to his audience, by the tone and nature of his arguments, by our knowledge of the eighteenth-century political scene, and by contemporary references to his pamphlets and their reception, we may identify as Swift's primary audience the group composed of the smaller country squires and the clergy and freeholders whose political behavior such squires dominated. Though threatened by the growth of large estates and the inroads of men of commercial wealth, the members of the lesser rural gentry in Swift's day still retained the greater part of the decisive political power that had long been theirs, and it was largely in hopes of influencing their use of that political power that Swift composed his tracts in defense of the Harley–St. John ministry.

A Short

CHARACTER

O F

His Ex. *T. E.* of *W.*

L. L. of *I*———.

W I T H

An Account of some smaller Facts, during His Government, which will not
be put into the Articles of Impeach-
ment.

L O N D O N:

Printed for *William Coryton*, Bookseller, at the
Black-Swan on *Ludgate-hill.* 1711.

Title page of Swift's Short Character of Wharton
Reproduced by permission of the Huntington Library

Three: Swift's Tory Rhetoric

Iᶠ in approaching Jonathan Swift's Tory political tracts I have been at some pains to indicate the political, biographical, and social circumstances under which they were produced, it is in an effort to do justice to the tracts themselves. A poem, a play, or a novel, insofar as it seeks to exploit a universal theme, is relatively timeless and can be enjoyed and understood with a minimum of outside reference. A work of political persuasion, however, once its timeliness has passed, is particularly vulnerable to misinterpretation unless we can at least partially recreate the specific contexts in which the author wrote. The relatively sparse critical attention directed toward Swift's tracts in the past has tended to focus upon either their value in furnishing evidence of his political sentiments or their usefulness as histories of the period. However, the bulk of Swift's political writings (despite his own occasional pretenses to the contrary) were not composed primarily as personal testaments nor yet as factual narratives. The immediate *raison d'être* of Swift's Tory pamphlets was the molding of public opinion for particular political ends, and it is in terms of these persuasive goals that the tracts can be best understood.

Two recent studies have amply demonstrated the important role which the formal study of rhetoric played in the education of a seventeenth-century British gentleman.[1] As a young man at the Kilkenny Grammar School and later in preparation for orders at Trinity College, Swift absorbed considerable training in the rhetoric he was later to apply to the Tory cause.[2] Though many changes in theory and practice had evolved in the two thousand years since Aristotle first formulated his rules for "discovering in the particular case what are the available means of persuasion," his *De Rhetorica* continued to maintain its place as a basic manual for the techniques of persuasive discourse. A familiarity with Aristotle and an awareness of his rhetorical principles are reflected in Swift's practice, and also in occasional references scattered throughout his works.

In his Tory tracts Swift is rather fond of ironically offering advice on rhetorical matters to his Whig rivals among the pamphleteers. The *Examiner* frequently takes the opportunity of criticizing opponents in their clumsy handling of appeals, and tracts like the *Importance of the "Guardian" Considered* and the *Publick Spirit of the Whigs* in essence add up to Swift's own rhetorical analysis of his enemies' techniques of persuasion. Of Aristotle himself, Swift wrote: "He writ upon *logick*, or the art of reasoning; upon *moral* and *natural philosophy;* upon *oratory* [i.e., rhetoric], *poetry*, &c. and seems to be a person of the most comprehensive genius that ever lived." [3] Whatever Swift's misgivings over the later variations and embellishments of Aristotelian doctrine, he continued to esteem Aristotle's own productions. It will be remembered that when, in Book III of *Gulliver's Travels,* Gulliver visits Glubb-dubdrib, he chooses to call up Homer and Aristotle from the dead, as well as all their commentators, only to perceive that the two sages were "perfect Strangers to the rest of the Company. . . ." [4]

In Aristotle's basic division the means of persuasion consist of either artistic proofs (those furnished by the author's invention) or nonartistic proofs (those external to art, such as documents). The artistic proofs are further subdivided into three kinds—the ethical (those appeals which establish the author's creditability), the pathetic (those appeals which play on the audience's emotions), and the logical (those appeals which are directed to the reason). In practice, of course, there are few proofs which fall exclusively into one classification. A pathetic appeal which exploits the reader's emotions, will frequently be of a sort which likewise enhances the author's character. In the same way, a show of logic may, under the guise of reason, include an appeal to fanaticism.

It is Swift's application in his Tory tracts of the various types of rhetorical appeals (as defined by Aristotle) which will be my concern in the discussion which follows. The validity or honesty of Swift's arguments will be treated only insofar as they cast light on his reasons for selecting one approach in preference to another. Certain of Swift's arguments, read in the light of what we know of the period today, may appear misleading or even dishonest, but this, with reference to his rhetoric, is largely irrelevant. Rhetoric, as the Puritans well knew, is essentially a Machiavellian art—it deals primarily with what is effective and only secondarily with what is right. Doubtless rhetoric *should* be applied only to lead men toward truth and morality, but, as Aristotle himself admitted, it *could* be and frequently was used for less exalted ends. I do not mean to imply, of course, that Swift's arguments were necessarily dishonorable ones, but merely to emphasize the truism that the criteria for judging rhetoric are different from the criteria we apply to logic.

Of all Swift's tracts on behalf of the Harley–St. John ministry, only the *New Journey to Paris* (1711) by "the Sieur du Baudrier" offers a fully imagined and consistent persona quite distinct from Swift himself. The *New Journey to Paris,* however, is more in the nature of what Swift would have termed a "bite" than a serious attempt at persuasion. When Swift turned his attention to more clearly political goals he made no sustained effort to disguise himself behind a fictional persona. In *The Masks of Jonathan Swift,* William Ewald finds that only the *Examiner,* among the important tracts, gives evidence of an "author" distinguishable from Swift, and even in this case, Ewald remarks, "the Examiner is so slightly individualized that one could argue that he is, in his fair attitude, really Swift. . . ."[5] But to say that Swift did not choose to assume an elaborate mask in his political tracts is not to say that he was at all unconcerned or casual about the picture of himself which his audience was to perceive.

The ethical appeal is one which no rhetorician can afford to neglect, for unless the character and good faith of an author are established in terms suitable for his purpose and his audience, his pathetic proofs, however moving, and his logical proofs, however convincing, are apt to fall on skeptical ears. Swift himself, in commenting on Matthew Tindal's *The Rights of the Christian Church* (1707), remarks, "although a Book is not intrinsically much better or worse, according to the Stature or Complexion of the Author, yet when it happens to make a Noise, we are apt and curious, as in other Noises, to look about from whence it cometh." He goes on to illustrate this axiom as follows:

For Instance, if any Man should write a Book against the Lawfulness of punishing Felony with Death; and upon Enquiry the Author should be found in Newgate under Condemnation for robbing a House; his Arguments would not very unjustly lose much of their Force, from the Circumstances he lay under. So, when *Milton* writ his Book of Divorces, it was presently rejected as an occasional Treatise; because every Body knew, he had a Shrew for his Wife. Neither can there be any Reason imagined, why he might not, after he was blind, have writ another upon the Danger and Inconvenience of Eyes. [II, 67]

In accordance with this standard, Swift does not hesitate to denounce his adversaries' politics by means of *ad hominem* arguments. In the *Publick Spirit of the Whigs* and the *Importance of the "Guardian" Considered* much of his reply to Steele's pamphlets is devoted to an attack upon Steele as an ingrate, an ignoramus, and an arrogantly presumptuous fellow. Swift's use of the "Character" (to be discussed in Chapter Five) furnishes many examples of his awareness of the fact that by discrediting his opponents as men, he could most effectively discredit their politics.

The eighteenth-century author's favorite method of seeing that his private character did not intrude upon the face he presented to his audience was the simple device of anonymity. Most authors, in particular those who wrote upon political subjects, both as a means of protection and as a matter of policy, left their work unsigned. In 1713 Swift joined in praising the defeat of a bill regarding taxation of the press, for, as he remarks in the *Four Last Years of the Queen:*

In this Bill there was a Clause inserted . . . that the Author's Name and Place of Abode should be set to every printed Book, Pamphlet or Paper; which I believe no Man who hath the least Regard to Learning would give his Consent to. For, besides the Objection to this Clause from the Practice of pious Men, who in publishing excellent Writings for the Service of Religion, have chosen out of an humble Christian Spirit to conceal their Names; It is most certain, that all Persons of true Genius or Knowledge have an invincible Modesty and Suspiciousness of themselves upon their first sending their Thoughts into the World: And that those who are Dull or Superficial, void of all Taste and Judgement, have Dispositions directly contrary. [VII, 105]

Whatever role piety and modesty may have played with the generality of writers, among the authors of political tracts there were more immediately pressing motives for anonymity. Aside from such things as fear of libel proceedings or of personal abuse, an anonymous author was more likely to receive a fair hearing than one whose biases and affiliations were known.

Guessing authorship was a popular coffee-house game, however, and few authors went long undiscovered. Although Swift did not affix his name to any of his political tracts, the anonymity thus conferred was, as we shall see, at best partial. He was widely suspected as the author of the *Examiner,* and by the time he had published the *Conduct of the Allies* and the later tracts, his authorship was generally recognized. Hence, he could expect that the criteria he himself had applied against others would be brought to bear in his own case—a case which was particularly vulnerable to such attack. Whig pamphleteers repeatedly pictured Swift as an opportunist who, having switched political sides in hopes of personal gain, now slavishly pretended to find all virtue among his new allies and all vice among his former friends. Obviously, the political pronouncements of such a man would be suspect. To forestall and answer such attacks—in short, to produce a more acceptable public face—was a basic necessity for Swift if his tracts were to persuade. Thus, while the political tracts contain no sustained persona in the sense of a created character significantly different from Swift, there *is* a distinct effort to delineate an "author" worthy of the reader's respect and confidence.

The *Examiner,* like all of Swift's political tracts, is written in the first person, with its tacit invitation to the reader to think of the author in personal terms. What is more, Swift shows concern that the "I" who writes the *Examiner* establish a character of some consistency. The *Character of the Earl of Wharton,* written in the fall of 1710 (just at the time Swift began his work on the *Examiner*) was of a size appropriate for an *Examiner* paper, yet the scurrilous tone of the *Character* would have been out of keeping with the picture of himself Swift was seeking to fix in his readers' minds, and so he chose to publish it separately. In *Examiner* 26 Swift tells his readers he has been serving the Tory cause for "half a Year in Quality of *Champion*" (III, 78), whereas actually, he had been the author only during the last three months of the *Examiner's* six months of existence. A reading of the *Examiner* papers which had appeared prior to Swift's authorship reveals that there is little or no attempt to disguise the Tory affiliations of the author.* Under Swift's pen, however, an effort is made to present the author as an involved, but unprejudiced observer of

* The first twelve issues of the *Examiner* were written by various men, among them John Freind, Francis Atterbury, Matthew Prior, and Henry St. John.

the political scene: he emerges an honest man, free of party affiliations and obligations, who feels constrained by events to speak his mind. The title of the paper he is writing presents Swift, as it were, with a ready-made pose to assume—he is an "examiner" of events, and he frequently makes reference to his title and function by italicizing the verb in his announcements that he is about to *examine* some specimen of Whig perfidy. He repeatedly emphasizes his independence, and bitterly objects to the inferences of rival papers that he is a paid hireling of the Tories. Swift opens number 15, his third *Examiner,* by affirming his lack of bias:

It must be avowed, that for some Years past, there have been few Things more wanted in *England,* than such a Paper as this ought to be; and such as I will endeavour to make it, as long as it shall be found of any Use, without entring into the Violences of either Party. Considering the many grievous Misrepresentations of Persons and Things, it is highly requisite, at this Juncture, that the People throughout the Kingdom, should, if possible, be set right in their Opinions by some impartial Hand; which hath never been yet attempted. [III, 13]

In number 29 Swift reminds his audience, "I am conscious to my self, that I write this Paper with no other Intention but that of doing good: I never received Injury from the late Ministry; nor Advantage from the present, farther than in common with every good Subject" (III, 91). Thus Swift repeatedly stresses the fact that he writes as a "Volunteer" who serves "without being called," and whose charges, far from being motivated by party malice, are "religiously true." There is, in certain of the earlier papers composed by Swift, some pretense of illustrating the author's "impartiality." In number 19 Swift admits that both Whigs and Tories have fanatics in their ranks, and goes on to claim that he has been attacked by extremists on both sides. The implication, of course, is that only blind partisans of either side could be offended by the *Examiner's* judiciously moderate remarks. In number 19 Swift goes on to assert that despite many urgings by extremist Tories, he refuses to increase the vehemence of his attacks upon the Whigs, for he is determined to maintain his careful impartiality.

Not many of his readers would be likely to accept seriously Swift's claim to detachment for very long; for the *Examiner's* "impartiality" is invariably displayed in such a manner as to cast maximum reflection upon the Whigs. Swift may, as in the cases already cited, scrupulously concede that a few Tories are overly bitter in their partisanship, but at the same time he makes it quite clear that *all* Whigs are dangerous fanatics. It would not take long for Whig readers to discover that although Swift pretends to find fault with both parties, it is only the vices of the Whigs that seem to occupy his attention. By the time he has reached issue number 41, while still proclaiming his lack of bias, Swift has become sufficiently confident of his readers' sympathy to allow himself the bold assertion that the Tory ministry's behavior has been *entirely* without serious faults.

I never let slip an Opportunity of endeavouring to convince the World, that I am not Partial; and to confound the idle Reproach of my being hired or directed what to write in Defence of the present Ministry, or for detecting the Practices of the former. When I first undertook this Paper, I firmly resolved, that if ever I observed any gross Neglect, Abuse or Corruption in the publick Management, which might give any just Offence to resonable People; I would take Notice of it with that innocent Boldness which becometh an honest Man, and a true Lover of his Country. . . . I know not how such a Liberty might have been resented; but I thank GOD there hath been no Occasion given me to exercise it; for, I can safely affirm, that I have with the utmost Rigour examined all the Actions of the present Ministry, as far as they fall under general Cognizance, without being able to accuse them of one ill or mistaken Step. [III, 152–53]

But while Swift, especially in the later *Examiner* papers he wrote, is not inclined to press any serious pretense that he is free of party leanings, he steadily insists, as has been indicated, that he is not a hired writer. Rather he presents himself as an independent private citizen, albeit of Tory convictions. Thus, in several issues of the *Examiner* Swift refers to the many letters he receives from readers suggesting topics for discussion and, by this means, lets his audience know that there is no person or group dictating his subject matter. In number 39 he replies with a characteristically indignant denial of the "tedious Scurrilities" of those who claim he is directed what to write. Swift devotes a good deal of space to answering the attacks made upon the *Examiner* by Whig papers, and these answers usually take the form of either lofty scorn for Whig "Hirelings" or expressions of sympathy for those poor wretches who, unlike the *Examiner* himself, are forced by hunger to write what they are told.

As has been indicated, the "impartiality" so boldly claimed by the *Examiner* is of a special sort. The *Examiner* is no detached observer judiciously standing above the political arena and calmly weighing the virtues and defects of each set of antagonists, for such impartiality implies a certain indifference, and Swift pretends no such lack of commitment. His impartiality is of another and higher sort. Both explicitly and by implication he presents himself as a man of fixed patriotic, religious, and moral principles; a man who has referred to those principles in surveying the political scene and has accordingly given his support to the party which best embodies them. If the author of the *Examiner* finds next to nothing worth praising among the Whigs and still less worth criticizing among the Tories, the reasons are to be found not in any vulgar party bias on his part but rather in his firm conviction as to where political virtue currently lies. Of party affiliations as such, the *Examiner* explains in number 43, he is contemptuous. His allegiance is to individuals and policies of virtue, not to factions of any one label.

The character established for the *Examiner* is significant, for it shows Swift in his debut as a Tory pamphleteer assuming most of the elements in the basic pose he was to use through most of his later tracts; although the varying purposes of the tracts and the different circumstances under which each appeared led him to make certain changes of emphasis and detail. The most important of these changes was to be reflected in the *History of the Four Last Years of the Queen* (1713). The face Swift presents in the intermediate *Conduct of the Allies* (1711) is in nearly all respects identical with that of the *Examiner* (1710–11), as he continues to assure his readers of his honesty, impartiality, and, most especially, independence. The political independence Swift claims goes beyond his mere assertions that he is not a paid propagandist. Although, as we have seen, he is not altogether consistent in his statements on the subject, in both the *Examiner* and the *Conduct of the Allies* Swift would have his readers believe that he is not even acquainted with the Tory ministers who, as he explains in *Examiner* 26, are so far from dictating his material that they have not even attempted to find out who he is.

In *Some Remarks Upon a Pamphlet Entitl'd "A Letter to the Seven Lords, &c."* (published in 1711 "By the Author of the EXAMINER"), Swift tells us specifically that he has no access to secrets nor any special private sources of information. Instead, he writes "nothing more than the common Observations of a private Man, deducing Consequences and Effects from very natural and visible Causes" (III, 195). The same pose is maintained in the *Conduct of the Allies,* where in the course of one three-page stretch he accentuates the public nature of his facts by prefacing them with the phrases, " 'Tis known enough," "every body knows," "But it was manifest," "It was judged," "It is credibly reported," and "it was said" (VI, 34–36).

By the time he wrote the *Four Last Years of the Queen,* however, Swift found that he had no choice but to drop the pretense that his tracts were merely "the common Observations of a private Man." After the publication of *Conduct of the Allies,* with its prodigious sale and political impact, the secret of Swift's identity could not be long contained. He had been suspected of being the author of the *Examiner,* and with the appearance of *Conduct,* nearly all doubts seem to have disappeared. The Whigs in their replies to the *Conduct* were not at all hesitant in ascribing it to Swift. Dr. Francis Hare, Marlborough's chaplain, in his *The Allies and the Late Ministry Defended Against France and the Present Friends of France* (1712) pointedly refers to the *"Swift* Pen" of *Conduct's* author (VI, xi). The Whig author of *Remarks on a False, Scandalous and Seditious Libel, &c.* (1712) is still more explicit, as he ironically remarks concerning *Conduct,* "The Spirit, the Language, the Honesty and Assurance of the *Examiner* are everywhere to be met with . . . the Prophaneness, which no Writer has lately err'd more in than himself, except it be the Religious Author of the *Tale of a Tub"* (VI, x).

With his identity now an open secret, Swift found himself the victim of a damaging personal attack designed to discredit his motives. The *Protestant Post-Boy* for January 19, 1712 (shortly after the publication of the *Conduct*), deals with him as follows:

One abandon'd Wretch, from a Despair of raising his Figure in his *Profession* amongst the Men of Distinction of one Side, fraught with Revenge and the Gleanings of *Politicks* which he pick'd up in exchange for his constant Buffoonery, and rehearsing merry *Tales of a Tub,* can best tell what glorious Fruits he has reap'd from his Apostacy, and Brandishing his Pen, in Defence of his new Allies, Against the D[u]ke of M[*arlboroug*]*h:* It must be a melancholy Reflection to one who has nothing in View but the present charm of *Profit,* to drudge on in *Renegado's Pay* without Murmuring, and from being the *Buffoon* of One *Party,* become the *Setting Dog* of Another. [VI, x]

In the face of such attacks, Swift could not blandly continue to maintain that he had no connection with the Tory ministry. His intimacy with Harley and St. John was too widely known. Swift chose instead to take the relationship his enemies called a vice and to advertise it as his special virtue. After the *Conduct of the Allies,* while still arguing (quite truthfully) that he is no Tory hireling, Swift becomes anxious to proclaim himself as a man whose comments are not merely personal opinion; rather he now openly embraces the role of semiofficial spokesman for the Tories—a man whose full knowledge of ministerial secrets gives double authority to his writings. This change in stance is signaled by *Some Advice to the October Club* (1712), written shortly after *Conduct of the Allies;* Swift's central point is his contention that the October Club's criticism of the ministry is ill-informed and hence invalid. "This Letter is sent you, *Gentlemen,* from no mean Hand, nor from a Person uninformed . . ." (IV, 74), Swift tells the October Club, and he goes on to hint that if he were able to disclose the high policy matters which he knows but cannot at present reveal, all carping at Tory behavior would be silenced.

By the time Swift composed the *Four Last Years of the Queen* (1713), the longest of his Tory tracts, he was even more anxious to stress his position as a Tory insider. On the opening page Swift announces that he had had "the best Opportunityes of being informed by those who were the principal Actors or Advisers" (VII, 1). In the pamphlet proper Swift further plays up his intimacy with the great and the resultant access it gave him to private documents and opinions. On several occasions he goes so far as to enter his own narrative as a player, casually using such phrases as, "I remember to have then told My Lord *Harcourt* and Mr. *Prior* . . ." (VII, 17), and "I remember when I mentioned to Mons. *Buys* [the Dutch envoy] the many Millions We owed . . ." (VII, 69), and so forth. Referring to a personal letter sent to the ministry by a prominent Dissenter, Swift remarks, "I did indeed see a Letter at that time from One of them to a Great Man . . . ," and lest anyone fail to notice his point, Swift footnotes this passage, "It was to the Ld. Treasurer himself" (VII, 21).

Originally intended for publication in 1713, the *Four Last Years of the Queen* was withdrawn because Harley and St. John felt that certain charges against the Whig leaders might cause dangerous repercussions. In

1737, long after the downfall of the Tories and Swift's enforced exile, he made plans to publish the tract but was once more dissuaded.[6] Final publication did not come until 1758, after Swift's death. Presumably, Swift first intended the pamphlet to be published anonymously, although as we have seen, his authorship was not likely to remain long undetected. By 1737, however, there was no longer any point in maintaining even token anonymity, and at that time Swift added a preface, under his own name, though he assures us that he made no other changes except stylistic ones. In this preface of 1737, Swift devotes himself almost entirely to an ethical appeal. In the straightforward manner of an applicant for a job, he presents his credentials, listing his qualifications for the task at hand; the points he chooses to spell out in 1737 are essentially the same ones he stressed by implication in 1713. They are (1) that he was in the confidence of the ministry, and (2) that letters and other secret documents were made available to him. Likewise, he repeats his assertion that he was no vulgar hack working in hope of money or other reward. This claim, which might well have been dubiously received in 1713, in 1737 came with double force from a man whose services had gone demonstrably unrewarded.

As we have seen, the pose which Swift assumes in his political tracts varies somewhat from pamphlet to pamphlet, yet there is an over-all consistency in his steady ethical appeal based upon his own claims to good faith. Even his protestations of detachment are not necessarily altogether inconsistent with his later claims of inside knowledge, for although Swift was intimate with Harley and St. John from the first, it was only in the later tracts that he made any considerable use of the special information they were able to afford. From the rather diffuse characterization of the *Examiner* to the more explicit and individualized author of the *Four Last Years* and the later writings, the character which Swift presents to his readers is essentially his own, but in an idealized version emphasizing in turn those features most likely to win him the reader's confidence.

Related to Swift's varying emphases in his ethical appeal are the differences in general tone and approach from tract to tract—differences which reflect the persuasive goals behind each pamphlet. One of the most noticeable of these shifts in approach is that in the *Conduct of the Allies* and the *Four Last Years of the Queen,* his two most ambitious efforts in the Tory cause, Swift makes almost no use of the satiric weapons he wields so successfully in the *Examiner* and several of the shorter tracts. In *Examiner* 38, after remarking that the law has many loopholes which enable cunning men to commit abuses that cannot be legally punished, Swift says:

I am apt to think, it was to supply such Defects as these, that Satyr was first introduced into the World; whereby those whom neither Religion, nor natural Virtue, nor fear of Punishment, were able to keep within the Bounds of their Duty, might be with-held by the Shame of having their Crimes exposed to open View in the strongest Colours, and themselves rendered odious to Mankind. [III, 141]

In keeping with this idea, Swift's *Examiner* papers are to a large extent satiric in tone, with a wealth of irony, parody, and burlesque.[7] Yet, by the time he writes the *Conduct of the Allies* Swift is sparing in his use of satire, almost never going beyond an occasional irony. With the composition of the *Four Last Years of the Queen,* he eschews it completely, telling his readers: "Neither shall I mingle Panegyrick or Satire with an History intended to inform Posterity, as well as to instruct those of the present Age, who may be Ignorant or Misled: Since Facts truly related are the best Applauses, or most lasting Reproaches" (VII, 1–2). Satire, as Swift's statement implies, is a handy and effective weapon for ridiculing one's enemies and discovering their faults, but in "an History" it would be out of place. A satiric historian would be a contradiction in terms: from a historian we expect calm instruction, and such cleverness or wit as he displays is an invitation to the audience to consider him as something both more and less than a sober historian.

In 1714 Swift applied to Queen Anne for the post of historiographer royal, in order "that the truth of things may be transmitted to future ages . . ." (VIII, 200). Though he never received the official post, Swift regularly maintained in his longer tracts the pretense that his objects in writing were to set the record straight for posterity and to supply information for such contemporary readers as were ill-informed. We need not doubt Swift's sincerity to realize that such a pose was well designed to enhance his readers' acceptance of his arguments. The plain-spoken "historian" who addresses us in the *Conduct of the Allies* and the *Four Last Years of the Queen* disdains the tricks of satire, for such techniques smack too much of what John Locke called "Rhetoric, that powerful instrument of error and deceit."[8] In assuming the role and manner of a historian and by making frequent assertions to that effect, Swift is offering his readers one of the most ancient and useful appeals of rhetoric, an appeal as old as the first speaker who told his audience, "I will not charm you with tricks; I use no art but merely let the facts speak for themselves." The difference between the sparkling pyrotechnics of the *Examiner* and the weighty seriousness of the *Conduct of the Allies* and the *Four Last Years of the Queen* results partly from Swift's discovery, after his initial experience, of the most effective stance from which to address his largely provincial audience, for the rural squire would be much more inclined to respond to the blunt, plain-spoken writer of "histories" than to the coffee-house wit who writes the *Examiner.*

Yet a paradox is involved in this change of stance, for it is precisely in those tracts in which he most insistently assumes the character of historian that Swift is most reckless in his attack. The note of disgust and indignation—already high in the *Examiner,* though somewhat mitigated by the laughter—reaches new heights in the *Conduct* and the *Four Last Years.* Marlborough, for example, is accused of nothing much worse than avarice in the *Examiner,* but in the *Four Last Years of the Queen* it is suggested that he had ambitions for seizing the crown. So vehement was Swift in his charges that, as has been mentioned, both Harley and St. John thought it best to advise against publication of the *Four Last Years.* Clearly, for Swift the role of "historian" did not in any sense involve an above-the-battle approach. His primary goal was persuasion, and all his efforts are in that direction. Only in *Some Free Thoughts Upon the Present State of Affairs, Memoirs Relating to That Change Which Happened in the Queen's Ministry in the Year 1710, An Enquiry Into the Behaviour of the Queen's Last Ministry,* and other tracts written either during or after the Tory collapse do we see Swift performing primarily as a recorder and analyst of events rather than as a polemicist. The *Publick Spirit of the Whigs* (February, 1714) is in reality Swift's final effort to influence public opinion toward the Tories.

Some Free Thoughts (composed May, 1714) and the tracts which follow do not read like political pamphlets at all. Not intended for immediate publication, they were written largely by way of reminiscence and apologetics. With the battle already lost, Swift's immediate persuasive goals were past, and he had taken on the job of explanation. Much of the baggage he found it necessary to assume as a rhetorician, he now dropped, and although he changed no basic opinions, Swift could in these later works afford for the first time to be candid concerning such things as the queen's unsteady loyalties and Harley's dangerous procrastinations. All this is done in a comparatively quiet, retrospective tone, though Swift's bitterness over the course events have taken is apparent.

The indignation which Swift displays so copiously in his longer public tracts is, in rhetorical terms, intended to develop and exploit his audience's sense of outraged patriotism. It is toward various aspects of this emotion that Swift makes his most sustained pathetic appeals. The picture he paints over and over again is that of a simple and honest John Bull intolerably duped and taken advantage of by unscrupulous foreigners. It is the special sin of the Whig leaders that, either through traitorous impulse or through hope of personal gain, they are actively helping foreigners to bring about England's ruin. This ruin is not to come through war or revolution, as might be expected, but rather through financial collapse, brought on by the Dutch refusal to carry a proper share of the war against Louis XIV. Thus the real danger to England, as Swift presents his case, comes from Britain's ostensible ally, Holland, rather than from her military adversary, France. Holland had been Britain's bitter trade rival much longer than she had been her wartime ally, and it took no special argument to convince a rural English audience, long accustomed to suspicion and mistrust of foreigners, that the Dutch had hopes for England's ruin. Most country squires would have agreed with Swift when he said of the Dutch (in the *Conduct of the Allies*):

. . . since we have done their Business; since they have no further Service for our Arms, and we have no more Money to give them: And lastly, since we neither desire any Recompence, nor expect any Thanks, we ought, in pity, to be dismissed, and have leave to shift for ourselves. They are ripe for a Peace, to enjoy and cultivate what we have conquered for them; and so are we, to recover, if possible, the Effects of their Hardships upon Us. [VI, 57]

The standards of shame are regularly invoked by Swift, as he asks his audience to consider how contemptuously the Dutch have treated the English. "What an Impression of our Settlement must it give Abroad," he remarks in the *Conduct,* "to see our Ministers offering such Conditions to the *Dutch,* to prevail on them to be Guarantees of our Acts of Parliament!" (VI, 27). Later in the same tract he comments, "I cannot forbear mentioning here another Passage . . . to shew what Opinion Foreigners have of our Easiness, and how much they reckon themselves Masters of our Mony, whenever they think fit to call for it" (VI, 33). The same theme, almost like a refrain, is carried out in the *Four Last Years* in such passages as the following:

It will have an odd Sound in History, and appear hardly Credible That in the several petty Republicks of single Towns which make up the States General, It should be formally Debated Whether the Queen of *Great Britain* . . . should be suffered to enjoy after a Peace the Liberty granted Her by *Spain* of selling *African* Slaves in the *Spanish* Dominions of *America*. [VII, 123–24]

In the *Examiner* papers Swift's appeal to xenophobia had not been restricted to contempt for the Dutch. In number 32 the attack on Harley by the Frenchman Antoine de Guiscard gives Swift occasion to remark:

I have sometimes wondered how a People, whose Genius seems wholly turned to singing, and dancing, and prating; to Vanity and Impertinence; who lay so much Weight upon Modes and Gestures; whose Essentialities are generally so very superficial; who are usually so serious upon Trifles, and so trifling upon what is serious; have been capable of committing such solid Villainies; more suitable to the Gravity of a *Spaniard,* or Silence and Thoughtfulness of an *Italian*. [III, 107]

In number 44 Swift gives special praise to the Tory repeal of the general naturalization act, whereby Palatine refugees who had been earlier admitted to England were now expelled. Swift hails the expulsion, explaining that the Palatines, "besides infesting our Streets, bred contagious Diseases, by which we lost in *Natives,* thrice the Number of what we gained in *Foreigners*" (III, 169). However, by the time he wrote the *Conduct of the Allies* and the *Four Last Years of the Queen,* when Holland's opposition had proved to be one of the major impediments in the way of a peace, Swift had narrowed his focus to concentrate mainly on the Dutch, though his attitude toward foreigners in general as opposed to the English is reflected in his comment (in the *Four Last Years of the Queen*):

I have been assured by several Persons of our own Country, and some Foreigners . . . That in most Victories obtained in the present War, the *British* Troops were ever employed in the Post of Danger and Honour; and usually began the Attack (being allowed to be naturally more fearless than the People of any other Country) by which they were not only an Example of Courage to the rest, but must be acknowledged without Partiality to have governed the Fortune of the Day. [VII, 146]

Another aspect of Swift's exploitation of his readers' patriotic emotions can be seen in his treatment of the queen. To the Tory squires who made up the backbone of Swift's audience, the monarch and the royal prerogative were sacred things. The Divine Right of kings had been somewhat tarnished by recent history, but though the days of absolute rule were past, the loyalties which the tradition had engendered remained operative among large segments of the population. Swift's real opinion of Queen Anne and the role she played during the Harley–St. John ministry can be found in the *Journal to Stella* (see entries for December 8–29, 1711) and in his later pamphlets not intended for immediate publication. In his public tracts, however, Anne appears always as a paragon, combining all the royal virtues. The process by which Swift glorifies the queen involves a certain distortion of fact. The English monarch, as later eighteenth-century history was to show, had not yet been reduced to an apolitical figurehead. The king still had very considerable, though ill-defined, powers, if he wished to use them. Anne, however, was not a "strong" monarch, and except for brief and erratic moments, she did not choose to act personally as a directing political figure. Yet, in the picture Swift paints in his major Tory tracts, it is Anne, rather than her ministers, who is the instigating force behind Tory policy and action. Harley and St. John appear primarily as her servants, merely carrying out the programs which she has originated.

Such exaggeration of the queen's role was an important factor in Swift's pathetic appeal, for by maintaining the pretense that the queen was the originator and director of Tory policy, he could equate opposition to such policy with disloyalty to the throne. As Swift puts it in *Examiner* 23,

The Friends and Abettors of the late [Whig] Ministry are every Day publishing their Praises to the World, and casting Reflections upon the present Persons in Power. This is so barefaced an Aspersion upon the Queen, that I know not how any good Subject can with Patience endure it. . . . [III, 59]

Likewise, in response to Steele's criticism of Harley and St. John, Swift, speaking in the role of Queen Anne, says (in the *Importance of the "Guardian" Considered*): "My Ministers were of my own free Choice; I have found them Wise and Faithful; and whoever calls them Fools or Knaves, designs indirectly an Affront to my Self" (VIII, 19). Swift's efforts to play up the importance of Anne's role are indicated by the fact that he chose to give his longest Tory tract the misleading title of the *History of the Four Last Years of the Queen*. Actually, the tract merely covers the negotiations leading up to the Peace of Utrecht. Much more descriptive of the work's contents is the title under which it appeared in Dublin, *History of the Last Session of Parliament, and of the Peace of Utrecht*. However, it was much to Swift's purpose in this tract to picture the queen as the protagonist, while playing down the roles of her ministers. Thus, in the *Four Last Years,* Swift barely touches upon Guiscard's attempted assassination of Harley, telling us merely: "The Circumstances of . . . [the stabbing] being not within the Compass of this History, I shall onely [*sic*] Observe, that after Two Months Confinement, and frequent Danger of his Life, He returned to his Seat in Parliament" (VII, 77). Although Harley's stabbing by a Frenchman was a circumstance which Swift had exploited to good effect in the *Examiner* (number 32), in the longer tract he chooses to slight it lest a display of too much concern for Harley should push the queen out of the foreground.

There is, of course, an implicit danger for Swift in his pretense that the queen directs policy, selecting her ministers only to act as servants who obey her commands. In answer to Swift's claim that criticism of Tories was really veiled criticism of the queen, the Whigs could reply that their own recently deposed ministry had been as much servants of the queen as were the Tories, and that therefore by his own definition Swift's attack on the late Whig ministers constituted a reflection on the queen's management. To counter this reply Swift maintains that the queen was at once deceived and oppressed by the Whig ministers, who during their reign misled her with false information, neglected to carry out her wishes, and even threatened her person. Under the circumstances, says Swift, it is not to the queen's discredit that she allowed Whig rule to continue for so long; rather it is the measure of her greatness that she was finally able to reassert herself. As Swift says in the *Conduct of the Allies:*

Thus it plainly appears, that there was a Conspiracy on all sides to go on with those Measures, which must perpetuate the War; and a Conspiracy founded upon the Interest and Ambition of each Party [the Whigs at home and the Dutch abroad]; which begat so firm a Union, that instead of wondring why it lasted so long, I am astonished to think, how it came to be broken. The Prudence, Courage, and Firmness of Her Majesty in all the Steps of that great

Change, would, if the Particulars were truly related, make a very shining Part in Her Story. [VI, 44]

In this way Swift suggests that Queen Anne's irresolution was in reality restraint, and her final lurching action in ousting the Whigs is pictured as aroused royal ire finally driven to assert itself.

Swift does not limit his emotional appeals to his audience's patriotism, though it is in this area that he makes his most sustained pathetic assault. He also exploits such matters as his audience's presumed High Church loyalties, its aristocratic biases, and its anticommercial feelings. Yet, however insistent his appeals to emotion, Swift cannot safely neglect making a strong appeal to his audience's sense of logic, for as the *Letter to a Young Clergyman* advises:

If your Arguments be strong, in God's Name offer them in as moving a Manner as the Nature of the Subject will properly admit; wherein Reason, and good Advice will be your safest Guides: But beware of letting the pathetick Part swallow up the rational: For, I suppose, *Philosophers* have long agreed, that Passion should never prevail over Reason. [IX, 70]

If reason must be the touchstone, even in a sermon to the faithful, then it is doubly important in a political pamphlet. Accordingly, though his arguments are often basically emotional, Swift in his tracts always emphasizes his own rationality as opposed to the enthusiasm of the Whigs. Thus, in a characteristic passage of *Four Last Years of the Queen*, he discusses the Whig support of an act whereby Quakers would have been allowed to substitute a "Solemn Affirmation and Declaration" for the customary oath in civil affairs. Swift's response is warmly to denounce Quakerism as the "most absurd Heresy that ever appeared in the World," and to declare its members and supporters motivated by "foolish Scruple" and "Obstinacy." He then drives his point home by ending his attack with a comment that sums up the attitude implicit in his logical appeals throughout the tracts: "So absurd are all Maxims formed upon the inconsistent Principles of Faction, when once they are brought to be examined by the Standard of Truth and Reason" (VII, 107).

In keeping with this self-declared "Standard of Truth and Reason" is Swift's portrayal of himself throughout the tracts as a moderate occupying a political position between the Dissenters and Republicans among the Whigs on the one hand, and the Jacobites among the Tories on the other.

Swift's moderation, however, though he no doubt thought of it as such, is actually more apparent than real in those tracts he wrote for contemporary publication. In *Examiner* 15, at the opening of his career as a Tory pamphleteer, Swift first announces what becomes a frequent refrain in his other tracts—that he abhors fanaticism in both parties and will attack it impartially. Some modern readers of Swift have tended to accept this pose at face value, but the evidence in Swift's political writings contradicts such a view.[9] Philosophically Swift's position, whatever his contentions, was not a happy middleground between two extremes—he was much closer to the October Club in his sympathies than he was to any dedicated Whig. In the bulk of his pamphlets he is seldom even mildly critical of the most reactionary Tories, while Whigs, however moderate, come under blistering attack.

Naturally, Swift is at greatest pains to proclaim his moderation in circumstances where it is least evident. However, the nature of Swift's accusations against the Whigs hardly suggests moderation. In his tracts the Whig leaders are not presented as mere fools who act through ignorance or stupidity; instead they are pictured as nothing less than conscious traitors, motivated by avarice and ambition, and beyond the bounds of political morality. Marlborough is more than a miser—he is a would-be usurper; the Whigs are charged with hiring Guiscard to stab Harley; and Prince Eugene is implicated in planning a series of assassinations of prominent Tories. In many matters, particularly those relating to passive obedience and Church affairs, Swift seems to have been rather more partisan than the ministers he served (particularly Harley), and, as we have seen, the vigor of his attack and the recklessness of his charges in *Four Last Years* were great enough to lead both Harley and St. John to oppose its publication. Swift's general attack in his longer tracts is not designed to meet the enemy halfway, but rather to destroy him.

The vehemence of Swift's attack is dictated to a large extent by the equally violent polemics which Whig pamphleteers were leveling at the Tories. Rather than take the defensive, Swift chooses to answer in kind and steadily to occupy an aggressive role. For this reason he seldom deigns to answer attacks upon his accuracy, affecting always to despise his attackers—though his real reasons are indicated in *Remarks on the Barrier Treaty,* where he says, "I pity Answerers with all my Heart, for the many Disadvantages they lie under" (VI, 95). In the *Examiner,* Swift promises to reply to all serious Whig critics, but later he tells us that he can find no charge worthy of an answer. In *Conduct of the Allies,* he includes a note promising "that whatever Objections of Moment I can find in any of them [the replies to *Conduct*], shall be fully answered in a Paragraph at the end of the Preface, in the next Edition of this Discourse" (VI, 65). Yet, though there were numerous objections, and many damaging ones, Swift took no notice of them. On the rare occasions when he does undertake to answer Whig rivals, as in the *Importance of the "Guardian" Considered,* Swift immediately seizes the initiative with an aggressive attack upon his enemy's personality, literary style, and social background.

Thus, in practice the "Standard of Truth and Reason" under which Swift operates invariably helps him to find all virtues among the Tories and all vices among the Whigs—a fact which has led some commentators to suggest that the success of Swift's Tory tracts must be counted as a triumph of emotion rather than of logic. Dr. Charles Lucas, who edited *Four Last Years of the Queen* on its first appearance in 1758, felt obliged to remark in his Advertisement, "Every judicious eye will see, that the author of these sheets wrote with strong passions, but with stronger prepossessions and prejudices in favour of a party" (VII, 172), and Samuel Johnson, though himself a High Church Tory and inclined to sympathize with Swift's political position, says with regard to *Conduct of the Allies:* ". . . surely, whoever surveys this wonder-working pamphlet with cool perusal will confess that its efficacy was supplied by the passions of its readers." [10]

Johnson's comment points toward a circumstance discussed earlier in this study; namely, that Swift in his longer tracts was writing not for a hostile audience demanding to be convinced, but rather for readers already predisposed to the drift of his arguments. When Swift undertakes to win over the skeptical, as in *Letter to a Whig Lord,* his tone and approach, as we have seen, are quite different from the more polemical note he strikes in *Conduct of the Allies* and *Four Last Years of the Queen,* where he is surer of his audience's basic sympathies. But almost any audience, however inclined it may be to accept a rhetor's viewpoint, must be at least made to *feel* that reason dictates its opinions. Thus, though Swift in his political tracts does not actually need to win over a skeptical audience with step-by-step logic, he must, in keeping with his dictum in

Letter to a Young Clergyman (cited earlier), make a serious effort to couch his appeals in ostensibly sober logic. This is not to suggest that Swift habitually employs dishonest arguments, but merely to point out that, given his audience, scrupulous reasoning is less essential to the success of Swift's logical appeals than is the creation of a strong sense of demonstration.

Swift uses two main devices to produce this sense of demonstration. The more frequent is the technique wherein he assumes the manner of a lawyer carefully building up an airtight case for the prosecution. As often as not his logic is impeccable, but when it is not, his form of presentation (bolstered by his audience's willingness to be convinced) helps to create the necessary sense of demonstration. Thus, in orderly fashion, Swift will first describe a Tory act or policy, then state the Whig case against it (often very fully and fairly), then finally, with the air of a man confident of his proofs, answer the Whig arguments. By way of example, in *Four Last Years of the Queen,* Swift relates how Queen Anne in 1711 created twelve new peers (all Tories) to counteract the Whig dominance in the House of Lords. He then straightforwardly summarizes the Whig claim that "it was a pernicious Example set for ill Princes to follow; who by the same Rule might . . . become Masters of the House of Lords, whenever they pleased; which would be dangerous to our Liberties" (VII, 20). Having stated fairly the Whig objections, he proceeds to offer a refutation.

We know from the *Journal to Stella* that Swift had serious misgivings over the twelve-peer measure and felt it could be justified only as a desperation policy, but rather than assume so defensive an attitude, Swift argues as follows: (1) If a monarch wishes to be a tyrant, he seldom bothers to justify himself by seeking precedents; (2) when men become peers, they are just as zealous to preserve their liberties as when they are commoners; (3) it is the duty of a monarch to re-establish an equilibrium between the nobility and the people when one becomes too powerful; and (4) only such prompt royal action by Anne could have saved the House of Lords from the "Republican Principles" with which the Whigs had sought to corrupt it. The fair presentation of the Whig case, followed by the point-by-point answer is designed to produce the effect of a faulty argument successfully demolished by one logically ordered. If we examine Swift's four points, however, we find that he has begged the question. His first two points prove merely that the mass creation of peers need not always result in evil, and his last two points, while possibly in themselves valid, are irrelevant to the question of whether a dangerous precedent has been established. A Whig or politically neutral reader would certainly challenge the logic of such a reply, but the rural squires who shared Swift's basic assumption would come away with the feeling that another Whig slander had been rationally disposed of.

The sense of demonstration which Swift achieves in his longer tracts depends on more, however, than an orderly charge-and-rebuttal procedure. In keeping with his pretenses as a historian and as a man with access to special information, Swift packs the *Four Last Years of the Queen,* and to a lesser extent, the *Conduct of the Allies,* with documentation intended to give weight and support to his case. The man who elsewhere so effectively satirizes pedantry here uses a good deal of pedantic apparatus, as he prints lengthy excerpts or paraphrases from treaties or Parliamentary resolutions. A few of the documents Swift thus quotes at length are confidential papers the ministry had made available to him, but by far the greater number had already been made public. He admits himself in *Four Last Years* that Sir Thomas Hanmer's fourteen-page resolution concerning the Allies is "already Printed" and that Queen Anne's five-page address to Parliament "hath been already in most hands." Nevertheless, he cannot forbear to include them. In a printed text of 166 pages *Four Last Years of the Queen* has approximately 32 pages, or one fifth of the total, devoted to either direct quotation or paraphrase of documents. *Conduct of the Allies* has fewer quotations, but almost as much space proportionally is given over to paraphrase and summary of what Aristotle would call nonartistic proofs, since documentary material lies outside the rhetor's immediate area of invention.

It is the heavy use of such material that Johnson refers to (in the same opinion cited earlier) when he says that the *Conduct* "operates by the mere weight of facts," though we may disagree with him when he says that they operate "with very little assistance from the hand that produced them." As any reader of scholarly books knows, the very dullness which copious documentation produces is an important factor in the desired effect, in which it is less important that the reader's immediate interest be held than that he receive a strong impression of painstaking research. A characteristic use of documentation for such an effect occurs in *Four Last*

Years of the Queen when Swift, in order "to avoid Mistakes upon a Subject where I am not very well versed . . ." (VII, 71), gives verbatim a four-hundred-word account written by Sir John Blunt concerning the growth of England's national debt. In *Conduct of the Allies* and elsewhere in his tracts Swift had already shown himself quite capable of giving a clear and even comparatively lively exposition of the same topic. Blunt's account, on the other hand, is totally concerned with figures, interest rates, and financial terms. Many readers, Swift surely knew, would be inclined to skip over so technical a passage, but by its very inclusion he adds a tone of authority and demonstration to his discussion. Modern students of Swift have noted his manipulation of figures and sums (as in the *Modest Proposal*) to achieve an ironic verisimilitude in his satire. In much the same way, by quoting Blunt at length, Swift for nonsatiric purposes is exploiting the average lay reader's instinctive respect for statistical demonstration.

One irrefutable standard for judging the effectiveness of rhetorical discourse is its reception by the audience for which it was intended. Of the tracts Swift intended for the public, the posthumous *Four Last Years of the Queen* admits no such test, but the success of the *Examiner* papers, the *Conduct of the Allies,* and the numerous smaller tracts, is well attested. This success points up how skillfully Swift made his selection from among "the available means of persuasion." As we have seen, Swift, despite his self-declared "moderation," was above all an aggressive polemicist much more interested in attacking his enemies than in proselytizing them. When, in such works as *Letter to a Whig Lord* and *Some Advice to the October Club,* he does temporarily assume a missionary function, the pose seems uncongenial and quite out of character with his customary role. It is significant that both of these latter works, as Swift himself admits in the *Journal to Stella,* had a disappointing reception. To the Tory squires and rural clergy who composed his usual audience, Swift served as a vigorous champion formulating arguments, clearing up doubts, and reinforcing convictions. More than any other single factor, it was this audience—with its dislike of foreigners, its traditionalism, its economic and religious origins, its patriotism, and its concern for order—that dictated the ethical, pathetic, and logical appeals of Swift's major Tory tracts.

Four: The "Several Ways . . .
of Abusing One Another"

I N his attack on Steele in the *Importance of the "Guardian"*
Considered, Swift tells the Bailiff of Stockbridge (to whom the pamphlet
is ostensibly addressed):

You must know, Sir, that we have several Ways here of abusing one another,
without incurring the Danger of the Law. First, we are careful never to print
a Man's Name out at length; but as I do that of Mr. *St———:* So that although
every Body alive knows whom I mean, the Plaintiff can have no Redress in
any Court of Justice. Secondly, by putting Cases; Thirdly, by Insinuations;
Fourthly, by celebrating the Actions of others, who acted directly contrary to
the Persons we would reflect on; Fifthly, by Nicknames, either commonly
known or stamp'd for the purpose, which every Body can tell how to apply.[1]

The list Swift offers, while by no means complete, does in general terms
cover a considerable range of rhetorical approaches, and it may serve us as
a convenient framework in which to consider Swift's own use of those
techniques which, as he amiably admits, were the common coin of all
contemporary polemicists.[2]

   Of the items in Swift's catalogue, the first (the use of blank letters in
names) and the last (the use of nicknames) are those which require least
comment. To spell out a man's name in a political tract was to risk
prosecution for libel, and consequently among eighteenth-century pamphleteers the convention by which vowels or all letters after the initial
consonants were represented by dashes was almost universally observed.
Swift's use of blank names was in no way exceptional. Aside from a few
names used in a neutral or flattering context, all the names appearing in
the tracts Swift published during the Tory ministry appeared in this form.
The only Tory tract of Swift's to be printed with the names intact was the
posthumously published *History of the Four Last Years of the Queen.* By

1758, when this work finally reached the public, nearly all the principal actors in the struggle for the Peace of Utrecht were dead, and Andrew Millar felt safe enough to publish the work with full names included, though at the same time Dr. Charles Lucas, who edited the work, felt obliged to insert an apologetic "Advertisement" in which he disassociated himself from Swift's "strong passions . . . [and] stronger prepossessions and prejudices in favour of a party" (VII, 172).

Swift occasionally chafes at the necessity for "disguising" his targets, as in *Examiner* 18, where he ends an account of Whig perfidy by saying: ". . . I should be glad the Authors Names were conveyed to future Times along with their Actions. For, although the present Age may understand well enough the little Hints we give . . . ; yet this will all be lost to the next" (III, 32). He then goes on to urge readers in succeeding ages "to consult Annals . . . in order to find out what *Names* were then intrusted with the Conduct of Affairs. . . ." However, Swift's concern lest posterity be left in the dark need not be taken too seriously. As he himself readily admits, the concealment afforded by such devices seldom misled contemporaries, and now as then, few readers of Swift's tracts would find it difficult to identify such figures as the "Duke of M-rlb." or the "Earl of G-d-lph-n."

Swift's use of nicknames in his tracts is infrequent. This form of ridicule would have been out of keeping with his pose as a sober historian in the longer pamphlets, though in the brief tract called the *Hue and Cry After Dismal* (1712) and once or twice in the *Examiner* Swift does use nicknames against his opponents. The Earl of Nottingham, "by reason of his *dark* and *dismal* Countenance," had been dubbed "Dismal" by the Tories, whose ranks he had left to join the Whigs. In the *Hue and Cry After Dismal,* published as a penny broadsheet, Swift describes Dismal and his servant, grotesquely disguised as chimneysweeps, discovered in Dunkirk, where they have gone to spy for the Whigs. The nickname "Dismal," which Swift was also to apply to Nottingham in his verse, is emphasized by being printed in heavy Gothic letters.

This attack on Nottingham is the only occasion in all his Tory tracts where Swift makes extended use of nicknames. There is a brief passage in *Examiner* 17 in which he draws a series of analogies for England's sad condition. Among other things, he compares England to a landlord cheated by his rent collector, *"Mr. Oldfox"* (Lord Godolphin—who in

1709 had been attacked in a sermon by Sacheverell as "Volpone"); by his clerks, "Charles" (Earl of Sunderland) and "Harry" (Henry Boyle); and by his seneschal, *"Will Bigamy"* (Lord Cowper). Lest any reader be uncertain of the application of these names, when the *Examiner* came to be published in book form the real name of each victim (though with letters missing) was given in a footnote. However, there is no attempt to elaborate upon these nicknames, nor does Swift use them elsewhere. Cicero's speech against "Verres" (Wharton) in *Examiner* 17 and the letter to "Crassus" (Marlborough) in *Examiner* 27, while both involve nicknames, are more properly examples of allegory and historical analogy than of straightforward ridicule by nicknames.

Listed second in Swift's category of polemical techniques is that which he called "putting Cases." In this phrase he seems to include a good deal more than simple argument by supposition. Swift's usage indicates that in the pamphleteer's sense of the words, "putting Cases" is meant to cover all argument by invented parallels. Thus, into this category fall such varying devices as illustrative anecdotes, allegories, and the whole range of analogy through metaphor and simile. Historical analogy, being based presumably on fact rather than invention, is given a separate place in Swift's list.[3]

As a defender of the party in office, Swift naturally, in the few cases where he offers extended supposition, tends to ask his readers to join him in considering what the Whigs might be expected to do if they were given the power for which they clamor. Thus, in *Examiner* 25, after proposing to explore "what the Consequences would be, upon Supposition that the *Whigs* were now restored to their Power," he suggests that "[in order] to give the Reader a stronger Imagination of such a Scene, let me represent the Designs of some Men, lately endeavoured and projected; in the Form of a Paper of Votes" (III, 71). What follows is an imaginary list of bills, petitions, and resolutions the reinstated Whigs might be expected to introduce. The list is interesting in that Swift, as his basis for each item, takes an acknowledged Whig principle or policy, but then proceeds to carry it one step beyond Whig professions, and thus into the realm of what his audience would consider shocking extremism.

He starts out soberly enough with a bill for repealing the sacramental test. The Whigs, whose professed toleration of Dissenters far exceeded that of the Tories, had already made efforts in this direction and might well do so again. But, building upon the basis of this plausible conjecture, Swift next has his Whig Parliament go so far as to bring in a "Bill for qualifying *Atheists, Deists* and *Socinians,* to serve their Country in any Employment, Ecclesiastical, Civil, or Military." In a like manner, Whig opposition to the doctrine of passive obedience to the crown (a doctrine about which Swift had his own misgivings) is expressed in terms of a bill to "forbid the Clergy preaching certain Duties in Religion, especially *Obedience to Princes.*" Or again, the plausible idea that the Whigs might well introduce a measure to make Marlborough a general for life is stretched to include the condition that "Care . . . be taken to make the War last as long as the Life of the said General."

A somewhat similar method is followed in *Examiner* 35, only in this instance Swift is more explicit in his technique of determining Whig principles by logically extending Whig professions one step further. He asks the reader to suppose that the queen, determined to end party strife, has ordered "the Principles on both Sides to be fairly laid before her" (III, 123 ff.). He then represents the Whig case as it might be presented by a champion of that party. What follows is a relatively fair representation of Whig principles, though Swift does not pass up the opportunity to state certain items in an unflatteringly bald and unqualified manner, as when he says, for example, that the Whigs "do not think the *Prerogative* to be yet sufficiently limited," or that "They see no Necessity at all that there should be a National Faith." At the end of his list, Swift remarks that he has "placed [Whig principles] on Purpose, in the same Light which [they] themselves do, in the very Apologies they make for what we accuse them of." However, he goes on to say, if we wish to have an accurate picture of Whig policy, "we should add other Opinions, which . . . are no more than what a Prince might reasonably expect, as the natural Consequence of those avowed Principles." With this in view, Swift is now able to point out that Whig toleration of Dissenters is in practice really designed to encourage atheism and that Whig desire to limit the royal prerogative is actually the first step in a planned return to the Commonwealth. The advantages of such a technique are manifest. Plausibility is gained by the fact that each accusation is based upon a logical extension of a professed Whig policy. By such a method, even the mildest Whigs may be pictured as dangerous fanatics, seemingly on the basis of their own words and actions.

In Swift's practice of "putting Cases" such supposititious argument is
less frequent than his use of illustrative anecdotes. Much in the manner of
a preacher, who enlivens his text with object lessons, Swift offers anecdotal
analogies to dramatize his case at the Whigs' expense. These are most
often brief and in some instances are not properly anecdotes at all, but
rather lengthy similes (to be discussed below under "imagery"). The
form which these illustrative anecdotes take is the one traditional among
orators: the subject under discussion reminds the speaker of an analogous
situation, either in literature or his own experience; he briefly outlines the
scene and concludes his anecdote on the witty line which points up the
story's application to his main subject. The following selection of such
illustrative anecdotes (mostly from the *Examiner*) displays Swift's typical
technique. Re: The high ambitions of a general like Marlborough:

It puts me in Mind of a Dialogue in *Lucian,* where *Charon* wafting . . . [a
general] over *Styx,* ordered him to strip off his Armour and fine Cloaths, yet
still thought him too heavy; *but,* said he, *put off likewise that Pride and
Presumption; those high swelling Words, and that vain Glory;* because they
were of no Use on the other Side the Water. [III, 45–46]

Re: How liberally the Whigs paid their pamphleteers:

I remember a *Fanatick* Preacher, who was inclined to come into the *Church,*
and take Orders; but upon mature Thoughts was diverted from that Design,
when he considered that the Collections of the *Godly* were a much heartier
and readier Penny, than he could get by wrangling for Tythes. [III, 75]

Re: Whig complaints over Tory attacks:

It is, I think, a known Story of a Gentleman who fought another for calling
him *Son of a Whore;* but his Mother desired her Son to make no more
Quarrels upon that Subject, *because it was true.* [III, 90]

Re: The danger of asking foreign princes to help guarantee Britain's
royal succession:

I remember there was a parcel of Soldiers who robbed a Farmer of his
Poultry, and then made him wait at Table while they devoured his Victuals,
without giving him a Morsel; and upon his Expostulating, had only for
Answer, *Why, Sirrah, are not we come here to protect you?* [VI, 94]

Such brief, aphoristic anecdotes, used to make a quick point and then
abandoned, are characteristic of Swift. The illustrative anecdotes that tend

to rely on pictorial rather than purely verbal effects I have chosen to include in my discussion of imagery.

There is, however, at least one anecdote which is of special interest. Swift customarily introduces his anecdotes with a phrase such as "I remember," or "I have heard." Occasionally, especially in the *Four Last Years of the Queen* (where he is anxious to indicate his position at the center of affairs) he will even intrude so far as to preface remarks with a phrase like, "The Lord Treasurer at that Time said to me. . . ." In one story Swift offers, however, he himself is an actor, albeit in a minor supporting role. In *Examiner* 15, after remarking on the Whig pamphleteers' fondness for quibbling disputes, Swift says:

> Upon this Occasion, I cannot forbear a short Story of a *Fanatick Farmer,* who lived in my Neighbourhood, and was so great a Disputant in Religion, that the Servants in all the Families thereabouts, reported, how he had confuted the Bishop and all his Clergy. I had then a Footman who was fond of reading the Bible; and I borrowed a Comment for him, which he studied so close, that in a Month or two I thought him a Match for the *Farmer.* They disputed at several Houses, with a Ring of Servants and other People always about them; where *Ned* explained his Texts so full and clear, to the Capacity of his Audience, and shewed the Insignificancy of his Adversary's Cant, to the meanest Understanding; that he got the whole Country of his Side, and the Farmer was cured of his Itch of Disputation for ever after. [III, 15]

This story is worth examination because it reflects certain basic attitudes on the part of Swift—attitudes he expresses on the assumption that his readers will share them. In tone, the anecdote has an element of the mock heroic and reads rather like a sketch for a scene in *Hudibras* or some similar mock epic. The story is not told in elevated language, but the very concept of a farmer and a footman disputing fine points of theology while cheered on by a "Ring of Servants" contains a mock-heroic contrast—in this case, the discrepancy between the dignified subject matter and the boorish disputants. Yet the footman, whom Swift has trained (much, we gather, as one might train a horse for a race), explains his texts "so full and clear, to the Capacity of his Audience," that he deservedly wins the contest over a man who had reportedly triumphed over "the Bishop and all his Clergy." Thus, there are two implications to this story, reflecting two different, but not necessarily contradictory viewpoints. The first, which is the major point Swift, as a Churchman, wishes to make, is that the truths of religion, when examined honestly, will be apparent even to the meanest intellect. The second implication, which mirrors Swift's attitude as an educated gentleman, is that there is nevertheless something inherently incongruous in the idea of servants and farmers engaging in theological debate.

Although in the *Four Last Years of the Queen* Swift promises to include no "Panegyrick or Satire with an History intended to inform Posterity," in his shorter tracts he is less concerned with posterity and sometimes chooses to "put Cases" in the form of satiric allegories. These allegories are of two sorts—those which involve personifications and those which are based upon "historical" events and personages. Of the first sort, there are in the *Examiner* three examples: an "Essay upon the Art of *Political Lying*," "A Poetical Genealogy and Description of *Merit*," and a "Genealogy of *Faction*." These are all more or less straightforward accounts, in each of which the birth and career of a personified abstraction are briefly described. A *"Political Lye,"* we are told in *Examiner* 14, may sometimes be born out of a discarded "Statesman's Head," or it may be "born an Infant in the regular Way," but in either case, "when it comes into the World without a *Sting*, it is still-born." When full-grown, this "Goddess" dazzles her victims with a mirror in which "you will behold your best Friends clad in Coats powdered with *Flower-de-Luce's* . . . , their Girdles hung round with *Chains,* and *Beads* . . . : And your worst Enemies adorned with the Ensigns of *Liberty, Property, Indulgence,* [and] *Moderation.* . . ." "*Merit*," personified in *Examiner* 30, is a rather more prosaic figure than *"Political Lying,"* who seems to be a changeable monster alternately female and human or neuter and animal in form. *"Merit,"* whose parents were *"Virtue* and *Honour,"* is pictured merely as a young man plagued by a spurious twin, *"false Merit"* (born of *"Vanity* and *Impudence"*), who embarrasses his counterpart by exploiting their resemblance. In like fashion, *Examiner* 31 briefly relates the story of *"Faction,"* the deformed daughter of *"Liberty,"* who had earlier given birth to such fair children as *"Riches," "Arts," "Learning,"* and *"Trade."* All heaven is disrupted by *"Faction's"* trouble making, and eventually *"Liberty"* and her entire brood are obliged to go down to earth, where *"Faction"* has since been occupied in impeding the progress of her more respectable brothers and sisters.

Allegories such as these, based as they are upon characters bearing abstract names like *"Merit"* and *"Lying,"* are at best rather inexact weapons, though Swift leaves little doubt as to what direction he means them to be pointed. Yet, to Swift, as a practical polemicist, diffuse attacks upon political immorality were of less immediate concern than specific attacks upon individual Whig policies and persons. For such purposes Swift chooses to employ allegory based upon a supposed historical analogy, as in Cicero's oration concerning Verres (*Examiner* 17) and the letter to Crassus (*Examiner* 27). In the first of these Swift reduces Cicero's six orations against Verres (the Earl of Wharton) into one brief speech of five hundred words. In this speech Verres-Wharton is identified as "a Robber of the Publick Treasure; an Overturner of Law and Justice; and the Disgrace, as well as Destruction of the *Sicilian* Province" (III, 27). (Wharton had been lord lieutenant of Ireland under the Whig ministry.) After further berating Verres as an atheist and a lecher, Swift suddenly breaks off his oration, pleading that "modern Corruptions are not to be paralleled by ancient Examples. . . ."

In *Examiner* 27, Swift's allegorical tone is quite different. He tells us that had he lived in Rome at the time of the First Triumvirate he would have been tempted to write anonymously to the three rulers, telling each of them which of his faults stood in most need of correction, and he then quotes the letter he would have sent to Crassus (the Duke of Marlborough). Whereas in dealing with Verres-Wharton, Swift acts as a moralist condemning a man whose crimes are beyond expiation, his address to Crassus-Marlborough is written as from an acquaintance and well-wisher who is grieved at the vice which mars his great friend's character. Inevitably, Marlborough's major vice, as Swift sees it, is a degrading and pathological avarice. After a disingenuous listing of Crassus-Marlborough's "good" qualities (skill in "the Art of bridling and subduing your Anger, and stifling or concealing your Resentments," and so forth), Swift goes on to say that all such virtues are canceled out in the public mind by Crassus' love of money—a fault which could be cured "by one Minute's Reflection." After earnestly urging reform, Swift concludes his letter, saying, "The Moment you quit this Vice, you will be a truly Great Man," and then piously suggests that "Perhaps a Letter of this Nature sent to so reasonable a Man as *Crassus,* might have put him upon *Examining* into himself, and correcting that little sordid Appetite, so utterly inconsistent with all Pretences to a *Hero*" (III, 85).

As Swift admitted in *Examiner* 17, the device "of looking into History for some Character bearing a Resemblance to the Person we would describe . . . with the absolute Power of altering, adding or suppressing what Circumstances we please," was one at which an author "must have very bad Luck, or very little Skill to fail" (III, 26). If the victim and his defenders chose to object to such an attack, the author could always answer that they, and not he, had made the application. Thus Swift, in his *Remarks on the "Letter to the Seven Lords,"* replies to charges that he had slandered Whig leaders in the *Examiner* by remarking: "My Business in those Papers was to represent Facts, and I was as sparing as possible of reflecting upon particular Persons but the Mischief is, that the Readers have always found Names to tally with those Facts; and I know no Remedy for this" (III, 190).

Swift professed to be surprised and amused at the Whigs' readiness to apply his damaging allegories to themselves. He closes *Examiner* 19 (just two issues after his oration concerning Verres) with a brief story:

There was a great King in *Scythia,* whose Dominions were bounded to the North, by the poor, mountainous Territories of a petty Lord, who paid Homage as the King's Vassal. The *Scythian Prime Minister* being largely *Bribed,* indirectly obtained his Master's Consent to suffer this Lord to build Forts, and provide himself with Arms, under Pretence of preventing the Inroads of the *Tartars.* This little depending Sovereign, finding he was now in a Condition to be troublesome, began to insist upon Terms, and threatned upon every Occasion to unite with *Tartars:* Upon which the *Prime Minister,* who began to be in Pain about his *Head,* proposed a *Match* betwixt his Master and the only Daughter of this Tributary Lord, which he had the good Luck to bring to pass; and from that Time valued himself as Author of a most glorious *Union,* which indeed was grown of absolute Necessity by his Corruption. [III, 40]

After giving this story, Swift comments: "This Passage, cited literally from an old History of *Sarmatia,* I thought fit to set down, on Purpose to perplex little smattering Remarkers, and put them upon the Hunt for an Application."

This little anecdote and the use it is put to furnish a noteworthy example of Swift's peerless talent for eating his cake and having it too. Swift would have us believe that his only purpose in recounting this story is to ridicule and confuse the Whig opponents who are quick to read hidden meanings into every line he writes. Yet it would require no special talents of interpretation on the part of the contemporary reader to perceive that this passage cited "literally" from an unspecified source contains an unmistakable allegory of England's recent union with Scotland. Scotland, despite its large Presbyterian population, had always been more Jacobite in its sympathies than England, and had for a time even threatened to install the Pretender upon its throne at Queen Anne's death. After long negotiation, primarily in the hands of Godolphin, this threat had been forestalled by the union of the two countries in 1707. Accordingly, in Swift's fable, all but the dullest readers would immediately see that Scythia stands for England; the "poor, mountainous Territories" bounding it on "the North" refer to Scotland; the Tartars are the equivalent of the Jacobites and French; the corrupt prime minister equals Godolphin; and the "glorious *Union*" between the Scythian king and his neighbor's daughter stands for the union of England and Scotland, along with the merging of their Parliaments. Thus, in the very process of mocking his enemies for their haste in reading allegorical interpretations into his works, Swift takes the opportunity to deliver another such allegory as they complain of.

When, as frequently happened, Swift's Whig rivals used their own allegories and "conjectural" cases to abuse the Tories, Swift usually chose to ignore them rather than to give added currency to their attacks by attempting an answer. Yet on one occasion he did heatedly reply to such an attack. After Guiscard's unsuccessful attempt on Harley's life, the speaker of the House of Commons had given a speech in which he congratulated Harley and the nation upon their narrow escape. The author of the Whig *Medley* had, after recasting the names and circumstances, vigorously criticized the speech and the speaker. Swift's reply to this device was put in terms which must have raised an ironic smile upon the lips of those who were familiar with his own practice. In *Examiner* 41, he asks indignantly:

Does this intrepid Writer think he hath sufficiently disguised the Matter, by that stale Artifice of altering the Story, and putting it as a supposed Case? Did any Man who ever saw the Congratulatory Speech, read either of those Paragraphs in the *Medley,* without interpreting them just as I have done?

Will the Author declare upon his great Sincerity, that he never had any such Meaning? Is it enough, that a Jury at *Westminster-Hall* would, perhaps, not find him guilty of defaming the *Speaker* and Mr. *Harley* in that Paper? [III, 155]

And a few lines later Swift scornfully surmises that, if challenged, the author of the *Medley* would probably resort to that "old Evasion . . . that I who make the Application, am chargeable with, the Abuse."

The final topic I wish to consider under the general category of "putting Cases" is Swift's use of imagery in his political tracts. Of Swift's imagery, Samuel Johnson has said: "His delight was in simplicity. That he has in his works no metaphor, as has been said, is not true; but his few metaphors seem to be received rather by necessity than choice." [4] What Johnson seems to view as a vice in Swift's general practice is in his political tracts, at any rate, something of a virtue. For the purposes of a polemicist, it is far more important that simile and metaphor be vivid than that they be beautiful, and appropriateness of imagery is more to be valued than ingenuity. Swift's imagery in the political tracts is "received" in the sense that his metaphors and similes are seldom startling or inventive but rather are the products of the natural and even inevitable parallels suggested by his subject matter and his intended audience. It is indicative of Swift's singleness of purpose and his constant awareness of his audience that in a series of works written over a span of four years most of the basic images regularly recur (though, of course, with many variations) and that in terms of subject matter, they fall naturally into classifications appropriate to the experience of his readers.

Among the recurring images in Swift's political tracts are those which concern servants. In these, England is pictured as analogous to a private family lately victimized by a crew of thieving and incompetent servants who have only recently been replaced by others more honest and qualified. The image is so obvious as to be almost inevitable, and thus, in Johnson's sense of the term, it is a "received" image. It was common usage, even in official documents, to refer to the ministers of state as "servants" of either the monarch or the nation, and carrying the implied relationship one step further into a literal application required no special inventiveness. Yet, the servant image, as Swift employs it, is especially calculated to strike a receptive chord among the rural squires and clergymen who comprised the bulk of his readership. Employers of servants are traditionally much concerned with the petty thievery, insolence, and general incompetence of those they hire, and many a country squire, as he read Swift's vignettes of rascally servants and duped masters, must have nodded reminiscently over similar real or imagined incidents in his own past. There is, for example, the occasion in the *Remarks on a "Letter to the Seven Lords,"* where Swift explains the change of ministry as follows:

I will put a parallel Case. . . . I have a Servant to whom I am exceeding Kind, I reward him infinitely above his Merit. Besides which, he and his Family snap every thing they can lay their Hands on; they will let none come near me, but themselves and Dependants; they misrepresent my best Friends as my greatest Enemies; besides, they are so saucy and malapert, there is no Speaking to them; so far from any Respect, that they treat me as an Inferior. At last I pluck up Spirit, turn them all out of doors, and take in new ones, who are content with what I allow them . . . do what I bid them, make a Bow when they come in and go out, and always give me a respectful Answer. [III, 201]

Or likewise the passage in *Examiner* 27 where Swift describes Whig corruption in similar terms:

When a *Steward* defrauds his *Lord,* he must connive at the *rest of the Servants,* while they are following the same Practice in their several Spheres; so that in some Families you may observe a Subordination of Knaves in a Link downwards to the very *Helper* in the Stables, all cheating by Concert, and with Impunity. And, even if this were all, perhaps the Master could bear it without being undone; but it so happens, that for every Shilling the Servant gets by his Iniquity, the Master loseth twenty; the Perquisites of Servants being but small Compositions for suffering Shop-keepers to bring in what Bills * they please. [III, 81–82]

Such imagery (other examples of servant imagery can be found in *Prose Works,* III, 25, 41, 43; and VI, 43), though prosaic enough, is an eminently suitable vehicle for impressing an essentially prosaic audience.

There is a similar "received" quality to Swift's frequent images comparing England's economic state to that of a private family gone into debt through financial mismanagement. Put in terms of extravagant young heirs, ill-advised mortgages, and grasping usurers, the folly of Whig fiscal

* There is a pun in this phrase. "Shop-keepers" is one of Swift's descriptive terms for the new men of mercantile wealth whose growing influence was an important source of Whig power. Thus, the "Bills" which the corrupt Whig servants enable such shopkeepers to present are Bills of Parliament.

policies would become clear to petty rural squires, struggling to hold their own in the face of heavy war taxes. In his first *Examiner* Swift sounds this note, saying that as a result of Whig economic policy, "the Country Gentleman is in the Condition of a young Heir, out of whose Estate a Scrivener receives half the Rents for Interest, and hath a Mortgage on the Whole; and is therefore always ready to feed his Vices and Extravagancies while there is any Thing left" (III, 5). On almost every occasion when Swift is describing England's debts, the analogy to a private fortune is made. Early in the *Conduct of the Allies,* for example, he illustrates Whig war financing by saying: "It is obvious in a private Fortune, that whoever annually runs out, and continues the same Expences, must every Year mortgage a greater Quantity of Land than he did before; and as the Debt doubles and trebles upon him, so doth his Inability to pay it" (VI, 19). He resumes this theme later on, saying that to the Whig men of money, "Every new Fund . . . is like a new Mortgage to an Usurer, whose Compassion for a young Heir is exactly the same with that of a Stockjobber to the Landed Gentry" (VI, 53). Toward the end of the tract, as he celebrates the Tory accession to power, he extends the image, this time combining it with the servant theme: "It seemed, as if the young extravagant Heir had got a new Steward, and was resolved to look into his Estate before things grew desperate, which made the Usurers forbear feeding him with Mony, as they used to do" (VI, 56). (For further examples of such imagery see *Prose Works,* III, 6, 24, 32; and VIII, 50.)

As is appropriate to a man whose subject matter is the return of the nation to health after its near demise at the hands of the Whigs, Swift makes heavy use of the imagery of sickness and disease. In a typical metaphor along these lines, Swift tells his readers in *Conduct of the Allies:* "We have dieted a Healthy Body into a Consumption, by plying it with Physick, instead of Food; Art will help us no longer; and if we cannot recover by letting the Remains of Nature work, we must inevitably die" (VI, 58). Numerous similar examples could be given, as in *Prose Works,* III, 12, 17, 62, 76, 77, 130, 134, 187; VI, 125; and VII, 95.

Perhaps it will be sufficient here, however, to cite Swift's extended use of sickness and recovery as an image in *Examiner* 24. His subject, in this instance, is the emptiness of Whig hopes that the nation will shortly restore the Whigs to power. It is the Whig view, says Swift, that the Tory ascendancy "was only occasioned by a short Madness of the People, from which they will recover in a little Time, when their Eyes are open, and they grow cool and sober . . ." (III, 64). In short, the Whigs believe "that the People of *England* are at present distracted, but will shortly come to their Senses again." To test this Whig idea, Swift proposes to examine "the Causes and Symptoms of a People's Madness" and apply them to the present case. He points out that "Frenzies" are often raised in populations in times of revolution, and he cites England's Commonwealth as a "great Example of a long Madness in the People, kept up by a thousand Artifices like intoxicating Medicines. . . ." Yet, "the Malignity being spent . . . the People suddenly recovered," and sanity was restored. This case Swift sees as a parallel to the present one, in which it becomes apparent that the ousting of the Whigs is no "new Madness," but rather "a Recovery from an old One." Thus, Whig concern for the health of the nation is hypocritical, since only by the people's illness may they profit. Their behavior, says Swift (changing the disease in question from insanity to physical illness), is like

. . . what I have often seen among the Friends of a Sick Man, whose Interest it is that he should die: The Physicians protest they sell no Danger; the Symptoms are good, the Medicines answer Expectation; yet still they are not to be Comforted; they whisper, he is a gone Man; it is not possible he should hold out; he hath perfect Death in his Face; they never liked this Doctor: At last the Patient recovers, and their Joy is as false as their Grief. [III, 67]

With the change from Whig to Tory physicians, Swift concludes, England's sickness is on its way to being cured, though the "Remedies that stir the Humours in a diseased Body, [may be] at first more painful than the Malady itself."

Almost as frequently as they appear in the roles of thieving servants, evil usurers, and hypocritical friends, the Whigs and their allies show up in Swift's political tracts as "Card Sharpers" who have cheated the nation of its rightful winnings. Thus, in *Examiner* 18 the change in ministry is described as follows: "A Sharper hath held your Cards all the Evening, played Booty, and lost your Money; and when Things are almost desperate, you employ an honest Gentleman to retrieve your Losses" (III, 34). Similar card sharper images appear in *Prose Works,* III, 37, 90, 97, and 137. Perhaps the most elaborate of such analogies is that in the *Remarks on the Barrier Treaty,* where Swift explains why Britian, after ten years of success in war, is nevertheless near bankruptcy.

I have heard a Story, I think it was of the Duke of _____ who playing at Hazard at the Groom-Porters in much Company, held in a great many Hands together, and drew a huge Heap of Gold; but, in the heat of Play, never observed a Sharper, who came once or twice under his Arm, and swept a great deal of it into his Hat: The Company thought it had been one of his *Servants:* When the Duke's Hand was out, they were talking how much he had won: Yes, said he, I held in very long; yet, methinks, I have won but very little: They told him, his SERVANT had got the rest in his Hat; and then he found he was cheated. [VI, 96]

The four categories of imagery I have described above—those dealing with servants, private financial ruin, sickness, and card sharpers—do not in themselves account for all, or even most, of Swift's imagery in the political pamphlets.* However, because of their recurrence and emphasis, they may be considered the four controlling images of Swift's tracts. As has been said, these images, like the others Swift uses in his Tory writings, are not calculated to impress the reader with the author's ingenuity. On the few occasions when Swift does offer a strikingly inventive metaphor, it is apt to be almost overly-inventive for the squeamish modern reader, as when, in the *Publick Spirit of the Whigs,* he suggests that Steele's criticism of the Tories is "the Spittle of the Bishop of *Sarum,* which our Author licks up, and swallows, and then coughs out again, with an Addition of his own Phlegm" (VIII, 38).

In general, however, most of Swift's images appear in just the sort of metaphors that might occur to anyone dealing with similar material.

---

* Some of Swift's other prominent images are as follows: He compares the Whigs to serpents (*Prose Works,* III, 200; VII, 20), wolves (III, 63), dogs (III, 147), unspecified beasts (III, 9, 106, 141), shoplifters (III, 91), counterfeiters (III, 135), murderers (III, 195), and defeated soldiers (VII, 4). The danger to the nation is described in terms of attack by storm (III, 39, 65, 70, 158; VI, 62), fire (VI, 8–9; VII, 101), and robbers (III, 96–97, 166). The new ministry is described in images of an army (VI, 45), a man bearing a heavy load (III, 6; VII, 75, 76), and a captain of a ship (III, 68, 69, 189; VI, 76). This list is not intended to be complete, but the examples cited here, along with those in the text, give an accurate, if not thorough, picture of Swift's imagery.

Thus, their effectiveness is based not upon their ingenuity, but upon their very "rightness" and upon the careful inclusion of vivid detail. Few of Swift's metaphors take his readers outside the normal range of their experience, and within that range Swift is skillful at enlivening what might otherwise be dead imagery with well-selected minor touches. An example of this may be seen in the image (quoted above) of the sick man surrounded by hypocritical friends, hoping for his death. Swift does more than sketch the situation; he gives us the friends' bedside whispers, "he is a gone Man; it is not possible he should hold out; he hath perfect Death in his Face." More effectively than a dozen paragraphs of description, such detail brings the whole scene to life. Likewise, in the story of the card sharper who cheats the "Duke of _____," we are given much detail which, while not strictly necessary in the analogy Swift wishes to draw, is essential in creating a vivid scene in the reader's mind. Thus, we learn the name of the card game ("Hazard") and the place where it is played ("Groom-Porters"). Nor does the sharper who takes the money merely pocket it; rather we are told he sweeps "a great deal of it into his Hat." With touches like these, Swift manages to breathe life into images which in less skillful hands might merely be routine.

Third on the list of methods of abuse quoted at the head of this discussion is the category Swift titles "Insinuations"—a term covering those devices which hint at damaging accusations while technically avoiding direct charges for which the author might be called to account. Swift affected to scorn such innuendo, and he sometimes denounced rival pamphleteers who, as he felt, either from lack of courage or of honesty, chose to speak in hints rather than explicit terms. Thus in his *Preface to "The Bishop of Sarum's Introduction"* (1712), Swift takes Bishop Burnet to task, among other things, for a cowardly mincing of words. Swift quotes a paragraph in which Burnet remarks that the clergy "so that they may now support a luxurious and brutal Course of irregular and voluptuous Practices, . . . are easily hired to betray their Religion, to sell their Country, and to give up that Liberty and those Properties, which are the present Felicities and Glories of this Nation." This statement would seem, at first glance, to be straightforward enough, but Swift affects to find it intolerably euphemistic:

Let me turn this Paragraph into vulgar Language *for the Use of the Poor;* and strictly adhere to the Sense of the Words. I believe it may be faithfully translated in the following Manner, *The Bulk of the Clergy, and one Third of the Bishops are stupid Sons of Whores, who think of nothing but getting Money as soon as they can: If they may but procure enough to supply them in Gluttony, Drunkenness, and Whoring, they are ready to turn Traytors to* GOD *and their Country, and make their Fellow Subjects Slaves.*

. . . for my own Part, I much prefer the plain *Billingsgate* Way of calling Names, because it expresseth our Meaning full as well, and would save abundance of Time which is lost by Circumlocution. [IV, 69–70]

Likewise, in *Examiner* 40, Swift criticizes a fellow Tory pamphleteer for not having the courage to do more than merely hint at the nature of Whig machinations against Harley. Had he been writing on that subject, says Swift, he would "with intolerable Bluntness and ill Manners" (III, 148), have labeled every spade precisely a spade.

However, despite his protestations and his pose as an outspoken man who never deigned to veil his meaning, in practice Swift was far too shrewd a rhetorician to scorn the powerful weapons of insinuation. In Swift's hands, these range from relatively crude innuendo to subtle manipulations of language. Among the simplest of Swift's techniques of "insinuation" is that in which he hints darkly, in carefully italicized phrases, at unspecified but clearly implied charges. Thus, in a *Letter to a Whig Lord,* Swift first remarks that the Whigs, having been so successful in corrupting the younger nobility, need only wait until the older members die off, at which time they will control the House of Lords. He then comments: "Neither perhaps would there be any Necessity to wait so long, if *certain Methods* were put in Practice, which your Friends have often tried with Success" (VI, 126). The reference, in context, is unmistakably to assassination. Likewise, in *Conduct of the Allies* we are told that the Dutch, in addition to the normal cooperation due to any ally, have been able to rely upon *"other Powerful Motives"* (VI, 57) on the part of the Whig ministers. Almost the same phrase occurs again in *Remarks on the Barrier Treaty,* where we learn that only "very *powerful Motives*" (VI, 87) could have led the Whigs to conclude so disadvantageous a treaty. In both cases, the *"powerful Motives"* in question, with their damaging implications of personal ambition, avarice, and treason, are left to the reader to supply.

Another of Swift's characteristic techniques of insinuation is the device wherein he describes an action and then, as if merely surmising, suggests two or more "possible" motives to explain it. Thus, in the *Four Last Years of the Queen,* Swift, at the end of a discussion of the Parliamentary investigation of Marlborough's financial speculations, remarks: "This Process is still depending, though very moderately pursued, either by the Queen's Indulgence to One whom She had formerly so much trusted; or perhaps to be revived or slackend according to the future Demeanour of the Defendant" (VII, 67). The suggestion that the prosecution might be revived if Marlborough were to misbehave, coming as it does from a man who claims to write as a special confidant of the ministry, carries the force of an unmistakable threat.

In the *Conduct of the Allies* and more especially the *Four Last Years of the Queen,* where Swift's pose as a historian precludes any of the heavy satiric and verbal embellishments he uses so effectively in the briefer tracts, he regularly turns to scoring off the Whigs by suggesting alternate motives (usually discreditable) for their actions. In the *Conduct,* for example, he speaks of those who supported the war, either from "Opinion, or some private Motives" (VI, 15), and later he remarks that the Whig ministers who negotiated a bad treaty "know best whether it proceeded from Corruption or Stupidity" (VI, 25). In the *Four Last Years* we learn that Marlborough had "one of his Creatures (whether by Direction or otherwise)" (VII, 22) spread lies about the queen. Furthermore, Marlborough, upon his return to England from Holland, "fixed his Arrival to Town (whether by Accident or otherwise)" upon Elizabeth's Day, a traditional day for anti-Catholic rioting. "Whether this Frolick were only intended for an Affront to the Court; or, whether it had a deeper Meaning, I must leave undetermined" (VII, 28). Likewise Swift is not sure whether the impossibly stiff peace terms offered to Louis XIV in 1709 resulted from "the Imprudence of the Allies, or . . . the Corruption of particular Men, who influenced their Councils" (VII, 33), but in any case, he notes that Louis "either felt or affected . . . much Resentment . . ." (VII, 36) on that occasion. Nor is Swift sure of Godolphin's motives in so badly mismanaging navy funds while in office, for, as Swift says, "Neither could I ever learn . . . whether there were Policy, Negligence, or Despair at the bottom of this unaccountable Management" (VII, 72–73). When negotiations at Utrecht were finally begun, we learn that sermons were preached in Holland against Queen Anne, and Swift muses as to whether this was done "by Direction or Connivance"

(VII, 136). Finally, in a passage near the end of the tract, Swift says in another conjectural aside:

Whether such vain Hopes as this [that Queen Anne would soon die] gave Spirit to the *Dutch,* or whether their frequent Misfortunes made them angry and sullen; or lastly whether they still expected to overreach Us by some private Stipulations with *France . . . ;* Whatever was the Cause, they utterly rejected a Cessation of Arms. . . . [VII, 152]

Almost equally popular with Swift are insinuations of a somewhat different sort. The technique is one he himself describes when, in the *Publick Spirit of the Whigs,* he denounces Steele for using it. Of Steele, he tells us: ". . . his Respect for the Clergy is such, that he doth not *insinuate* as if they really had . . . evil Dispositions; he only *insinuates,* that they give *too much Cause* for such *Insinuations"* (VIII, 39). As Swift's description implies, the method is one where the author points out whatever causes for suspicion exist in a situation and then, carefully refraining from a direct charge, suggests that so much smoke must surely conceal some fire. Thus, in *Examiner* 32, while discussing Guiscard's attempted assassination of Harley, Swift pointedly asks:

If there be really so great a Difference in Principle between the *High-flying Whigs,* and the Friends of *France;* I cannot but repeat the Question, how come they to join in the Destruction of the same Man? Can his Death be possibly for the Interest of Both? or have they Both the same Quarrel against Him, that he is perpetually discovering and preventing the treacherous Designs of our Enemies? [III, 109–10]

Or again, in the *Conduct of the Allies,* Swift remarks that in all of the Allied treaties concerning the war there is almost no evidence of any concern for Britain's interest, then says:

Let those who think this too severe a Reflection, examin [*sic*] the whole Management of the present War by Sea and Land with all our Alliances, Treaties, Stipulations and Conventions, and consider, whether the whole does not look as if some particular Care and Industry had been used, to prevent any Benefit or Advantage that might possibly accrue to *Britain.* [VI, 24]

This technique, one of the oldest and most reliable methods of insinuation available to the political controversialist, is put to good use by Swift throughout his tracts, though there are relatively few places where it can be illustrated by brief quotation. It is in the general drift of his argument and in his whole tone, rather than in specific instances, that Swift most strongly insinuates that the Whigs "give *too much Cause for . . . Insinuations.*"

One of the reasons why Swift's friends so consistently advised against publication of the *Four Last Years of the Queen* was the extreme nature of certain charges it contained.[5] Two of the most startling of the charges were: (1) the suggestion that the Duke of Marlborough had ambitions toward installing himself upon the English throne, and (2) the claim that Prince Eugene of Austria had been a participant in an abortive plot to assassinate Harley. The second of these accusations, as we shall see, is made with a show of bold directness, but in the charge against Marlborough—a man much more likely to have warm defenders in England than was the foreign prince—it became necessary to resort to less overt means. The method Swift used is indicated in Charles Lucas' "Advertisement" to the 1758 edition. Lucas remarks that Swift "is not content with laying open again the many faults already publicly proved upon the late Duke of *Marlborough,* but insinuates a new crime, by seeming to attempt to acquit him of aspiring at the throne. But this is done in a manner peculiar to this author" (VII, 175).

The first faint suggestion on Swift's part that Marlborough might be chargeable with so daring an ambition had come in the *Conduct of the Allies,* where he comments concerning the duke's request for a lifetime commission as general: ". . . by these Steps, a *General during Pleasure,* might have grown into a *General for Life,* and a *General for Life* into a *King*" (VI, 44–45). Swift does not elaborate upon this idea, and the implied accusation can be viewed as merely conjectural. The more damaging insinuation appears early in the *Four Last Years,* after Swift has further prepared the way by announcing on the first page that he intends to disclose Whig designs not only against the Tory ministry, "but in some manner against the Crown itself" (VII, 1). Six pages later, while giving Marlborough's "Character," Swift finally, with impressive economy, fires his shot:

We are not to take the Height of his Ambition from his soliciting to be General for Life: I am persuaded, his chief Motive was the Pay and Perquisites by continuing the War; and, that he had *then* [that is, early in the war] no Intentions of settling the Crown in his Family; his only Son having been dead some years before. [VII, 7]

This is all; the charge, made almost casually, as if in an aside, is not repeated or referred to again. No actionable statement has been made, but the force of that single, carefully italicized *"then,"* introduced in a passage ostensibly clearing Marlborough of an unfair suspicion, suggests clearly that he was later to become guilty of a crime most Englishmen would view as combining the worst elements of treason and sacrilege.

Somewhat analogous to Swift's technique of insinuating serious charges while ostensibly denying them is his employment of apophasis,* that device wherein the rhetor brings up a topic while disclaiming his intention to mention it ("I will say nothing of his many crimes"). Apophasis furnished Swift with another weapon particularly handy against the Duke of Marlborough. Though his star was steadily declining, Marlborough was still a popular military hero at the time Swift wrote his tracts, and a direct attack upon his person might well have backfired. Apophasis— with its technique of abuse while denying abusive intent—was perfectly suited to Swift's task, and he uses it against the duke regularly (see *Prose Works,* III, 21; VII, 7). Perhaps his most elaborate apophasis comes in the *Conduct of the Allies,* where, speaking of Marlborough's avarice, Swift says:

I shall wave [*sic*] any thing that is Personal upon this Subject. I shall say nothing of those great Presents made by several Princes, which the Soldiers used to call Winter Foraging, and said it was better than that of the Summer; of Two and an half *per Cent.* subtracted out of all the Subsidies we pay in those Parts, which amounts to no inconsiderable Sum; and lastly, of the grand Perquisites in a long successful War, which are so amicably adjusted between Him and the *States.* [VI, 41–42]

Another device that Swift put to use is the reverse of apophasis— namely, pophasis—wherein the rhetor, after boldly announcing his intention to deal fully with a topic, subsequently fails to do so. This technique Swift employs in the second of the above-mentioned daring charges in the *Four Last Years of the Queen*—the accusation that Prince Eugene had conspired at Harley's assassination. In this case Swift, far from resorting

* In accordance with Swift's own frequent advice to shun esoteric terms, I have in general tried to avoid using elaborate technical names for rhetorical devices. However, in the present case I have chosen to use the technical term in preference to the sort of clumsy circumlocution that would be needed to replace it.

to innuendo, flatly asserts that the prince "proposed an Expedient, often practiced by those of his Country, That the Treasurer (to use his own Expression) should be taken off *à la negligence*" (VII, 26). Since so forthright an accusation (in which even the prince's words are given) requires a greater show of support than is necessary in the case of more casually oblique charges, Swift follows up by saying: "I am very sensible that such an Imputation ought not to be charged upon any Person whatsoever, upon slight Grounds or doubtful Surmizes; And, that those who think I am able to produce no better, will judge this Passage to be fitter for a Libel, than a History" (VII, 27). After so firm a statement, we expect that Swift will carefully back up his charge, yet he merely mentions that "intercepted Letters" (unquoted and unspecified) and an unidentified "Person who was at the Meeting" planning the assassination confirm the charge "past all Contradiction." The self-assurance of Swift's manner in presenting his "proof" helps to veil the flimsiness of what little "evidence" he has to offer.

Remaining for discussion is the item which appears fourth in the list of abusive techniques Swift cited for the bailiff of Stockbridge. This device Swift describes as "celebrating the Actions of others, who acted directly contrary to the Persons we would reflect on." Though Swift places it in a separate category, such argument by factual example is essentially a variation of "putting Cases," wherein analogy and comparison are always the basic elements. The suggestion of a contrast unflattering to the Whigs is implicit on almost every occasion in the tracts when the Tory ministry is praised, but Swift, relying to some extent on his audience's general anti-Whig bias, seldom finds it necessary or desirable to make such comparisons overtly. It is to history rather than to the contemporary scene that Swift turns when he wishes to attack the Whigs by "celebrating the Actions of others."

Perhaps the most effective of the historical parallels drawn by Swift is the comparison between "A Bill of *ROMAN* Gratitude" and "A Bill of *BRITISH* Ingratitude" made in *Examiner* 16. In answer to Whig charges that the removal of Marlborough was a shocking example of ingratitude to an almost uniformly victorious general, Swift undertakes to convince the world that Britain was "not quite so ungrateful either as the *Greeks* or the *Romans*," and accordingly he presents in parallel columns, as if in an audit statement, the respective rewards received by a victorious Roman general and by Marlborough. The "Bill of *ROMAN* Gratitude" is detailed and scrupulously exact, containing such headings as "For Frankincense and Earthen Pots to burn it in" (£4.10) and "A Crown of Laurel" (2*d.*). The most costly item is "A Triumphal Arch," listed at £500, and the total expenditure is £994.11.10*d.* Opposed to the meticulous detail of the Roman list is the "Bill of *BRITISH* Ingratitude." Here Swift deals only in round figures and huge sums, such as "Blenheim" (£200,000) and "Employments" (£100,000). Britain's ingratitude adds up to a total outlay of £540,000, and this sum, Swift tells us, is "but a Trifle, in Comparison of what is *untold*" (III, 21–24).

It is characteristic of Swift's use of historical analogy, as in the case just cited, that his examples are selected not so much to extol the wisdom of the past as to emphasize the unparalleled corruption of the present. Thus, in the *Conduct of the Allies,* when he considers the financial drains imposed upon England in all her wars since the Conquest, he can find no parallel to present conditions: "In the Civil-Wars of the *Barons,* as well as those between the Houses of *York* and *Lancaster,* great Destruction was made of the Nobility and Gentry . . . , but the Money spent on both sides was employed and circulated at Home; no Publick Debts [were] contracted." The same is true of "that unnatural Rebellion against King *Charles* I," and in the wars against Scotland. Even the "first Wars with *France*" ran up only small, easily cleared debts. Nor did the *"Dutch* Wars, in the Reign of King *Charles* II," leave "any Debt upon the Nation [or carry] any Mony out of it." It is only with the present wars against France that "the Custom first began . . . of borrowing Millions upon Funds of Interest" (VI, 9–10). And Swift returns to this theme later in the tract, this time having at last found a historical parallel for England's national debt:

'Tis wonderful, that our Ancestors, in all their Wars, should never fall under such a Necessity [i.e., a national debt]; that we meet no Examples of it, in *Greece* and *Rome;* that no other Nation in *Europe* ever knew any thing like it, except *Spain,* about an Hundred and twenty Years ago; which they drew upon themselves, by their own Folly, and have suffered for it ever since. [VI, 55]

Likewise, in a passage of *Examiner* 17, cited earlier, Swift breaks off his allegorical version of Cicero's oration against Verres, saying: "This Ex-

tract . . . hath cost me more Pains than I think it is worth, having only
served to convince me, that modern Corruptions are not to be parallelled
by ancient Examples . . ." (III, 29). Similarly, in *Examiner* 32, Guiscard's stabbing of Harley, we learn, is "not to be parallelled by any [act]
of the like kind we meet with in History." The stabbings of Caesar, of
Henri III of France, and the Duke of Buckingham are all examined, and
Swift decides that, allowing for the difference in degree between a king
and a minister of state, "this Attempt of *Guiscard* seems to have outdone
them all in every heightning Circumstance . . ." (III, 106–7).

In this brief survey I have not sought to deal exhaustively with the
infinitely variegated methods Swift employs as a polemicist. Rather, using
Swift's own catalogue as a guide, I have tried to indicate something of the
range of stylistic and rhetorical techniques he brings to bear in performing his function as a political controversialist. None of these techniques
were original or unique with Swift; but in the skill with which he selected
his weapons and in the vigor with which he wielded them, Swift had few
peers.

Five: Swift's Polemical Characters

IN his *Thoughts on Various Subjects,* Swift remarks: "Satyr is reckoned the easiest of all Wit; but I take it to be otherwise in very bad Times; For it is as hard to satyrize well a Man of distinguished Vices, as to praise well a Man of distinguished Virtues." [1] Difficult though the task might be, in his role as Tory propagandist during 1710–14 Swift found frequent occasion to practice the art of ridiculing "distinguished Vice" and (to a lesser extent) of praising "distinguished Virtue." In the *Short Character of His Excellency Thomas Earl of Wharton,* in the gallery of Whig and Tory leaders who figure in the *Four Last Years of the Queen,* and in random portraits scattered throughout his political tracts, Swift offered his readers a series of personality studies ranging in scope from the extended formal "Character" down to the one- or two-line sketch in miniature.

The Theophrastan Character, as popularized in the seventeenth century by Joseph Hall, Sir Thomas Overbury, and others, customarily dealt with nonindividualized personages, each designed to typify a definite moral quality or social role. Thus, a figure might be characterized as "A Jealous Man," "A Plain Country Fellow," or "A Worthy Soldier." What followed was most often a descriptive sketch, usually brief, in which the Character in question was illustrated with appropriate details of appearance and action. Though the Character-writers of the seventeenth century frequently wrote with particular men in mind, it was a primary requirement of the form that the subject, like the personified vices and virtues of allegory, be as generally applicable as possible. With this goal in mind, Character-writers customarily dealt only with traits that were relevant to the central quality they sought to describe. As the century wore on and the Character came into increasing use as a political weapon, the Characters of "A Hypocrite," "A Papist," and "A Minister of State" might merge into "A Hypocritical Papist Minister of State" unmistakably modeled upon a recognizable individual, but always under the pretense that a type, rather than a single person, was being described.[2]

Yet, for political purposes, as opposed to general social commentary, a Character description, whether intended for satire, invective, or panegyric, is always most effective when most individualized. To describe a man as merely one representative of a larger group is to diminish the degree of admiration or revulsion his Character is meant to elicit. In satire particularly, as Swift knew, a single, well-placed bullet is a good deal more lethal than a scattering of shot. Thus, in Swift's practice, the Character is nearly always a device for describing specific men, often identified by name. Each man is defined by his unique combination of qualities, good or bad, though Swift may sometimes, in reverse of the older process, picture an individual so dominated by one quality as to suggest a broader classification. In his portrait of Marlborough in *Four Last Years of the Queen,* for example, we may detect the outlines of "An Avaricious Man," but by the inclusion of biographical detail, Swift takes care to keep our main attention focused upon Marlborough the individual, rather than upon the type he happens to represent.

As a genre, the Character has always been basically more useful as a method of attack than as a means of praise. The thirty surviving *Ethical Characters* of Theophrastus deal exclusively with unpleasant types, and though the Character-books of the seventeenth century frequently sought to balance their portraits of vice with others of virtue, the Character (like the analogous Jonsonian Humour Figure) owed its vogue primarily to its effectiveness in describing the evil, the absurd, and the grotesque in men. From his Theophrastan predecessors Swift inherited the tradition of the Character as a weapon of attack. Even when circumstances of expediency or genuine admiration led him to describe a "good" Character, Swift was apt to find it most congenial to express his praise ironically as raillery.

This latter technique is apparent at the start of Swift's career as an author, in his dedication of the *Tale of a Tub* to Lord Somers. It had long been the custom for aspiring authors to dedicate their works to prominent men, whose good qualities would be celebrated in suitably admiring language. Judicious balance is not a cardinal virtue in such matters, and the writer of dedications, like the writer of epitaphs, was by tacit agreement allowed a considerable license with factual truth. It was not uncommon in dedications to find the most extravagant merits ascribed to men who in real life were of indifferent character, or even to see pictured as moral paragons men who were notorious rakes. In these circumstances it is not surprising that Swift, disgusted with the hypocrisy so prevalent in dedications, should have come to believe that "All Panegyricks are mingled with an Infusion of Poppy" (IV, 252). Though as a beginning author Swift could not afford to forego the opportunity of winning favor with so powerful a lord as Somers, he could at least offer his dedication of a *Tale of a Tub* in terms designed to circumvent the stale conventions of the usual panegyric and at the same time to satirize the whole form itself.

In writing his antidedication, Swift turned to what he felt was "the finest Part of Conversation"—namely, raillery. As he defined it in *Hints Towards an Essay on Conversation,* the art of raillery consisted in saying "something that at first appeared a Reproach, or Reflection; but, by some Turn of Wit unexpected and surprising, ended always in a Compliment, and to the Advantage of the Person it was addressed to" (IV, 91). In maladroit hands, the technique might emerge as mere "Repartee," wherein real insults were offered under a surface show of good humor; but, when skillfully practiced, genuine raillery offered a graceful means of paying extravagant compliments while avoiding the obsequious stance of the obvious flatterer.

As if to remove himself yet one step further from the role of sycophant, in his dedication of the *Tale of a Tub* Swift poses as a plain-spoken bookseller naïvely anxious to launch his product under suitable auspices. The impractical author, he explains, has dedicated his book to posterity, but he, the bookseller, is more conversant in the ways of the world, and therefore is sure that only under the patronage of a great man like Somers will the book prosper. The author, it seems, had written *"DETUR DIGNISSIMO"* on the cover of his manuscript, and the bookseller, having with some difficulty had the phrase translated as "Let it be given to the Worthiest," set about to discover who might be "the sublimest Genius of the Age, for Wit, Learning, Judgment, Eloquence and Wisdom" (I, 14 ff.). He says that each man he questioned selected himself for the role, but the unanimous second choice was Somers, and so the book is dedicated to him.

The bookseller goes on to say that, "being very unacquainted in the

Style and Form of Dedications," he employed a number of wits to compose an appropriate panegyric, but the one they produced left him dissatisfied, for it merely repeated the "old beaten Story" of Somers' already universally acknowledged superiority in every "Virtue, either of a Publick or Private Life. . . ." Besides, says the bookseller, it would be a disservice to Somers' posthumous reputation to eulogize him in a form so generally given over to lying praise; since "as Dedications have run for some Years past, a good Historian will not be apt to have Recourse thither, in search of Characters." In closing, the bookseller expresses his admiration of Somers' patient toleration of the sort of hollow encomiums usually directed toward him by the tribe of dedicators. Clearly, Swift's praise of Somers in this dedication, however obliquely addressed, could hardly have been more fulsome; its force is doubly enhanced by the fact that it appears in the guise of an attack upon just such fulsomeness.*

As Swift's career advanced, he was to resort frequently to the indirect technique of raillery when describing the Characters of those persons he wished to praise. His dedication of a *Project for the Advancement of Religion* (1709) to the Countess of Berkeley is similar in tone to the Somers dedication. While admitting to the countess that his purpose is "the very same I have often detested in most Dedications; That of publishing your Praises to the World" (II, 43), he prefaces his more direct compliments with mock-disclaimers of any awe over her noble family ("I know others as noble"), the size of her fortune ("I know others far greater"), and the beauty of her children ("even this may, perhaps, have been equalled in some other Age, or Country"). Likewise, in his private correspondence Swift more often than not prefers to frame his compliments in terms of raillery, as when, on June 13, 1709, he writes Lord Halifax:

---

* Swift's esteem for Somers (whom he flatteringly pictured in his *Contests and Dissensions in Athens and Rome* as Aristides, "a Person of the strictest Justice, and best acquainted with the Laws, as well as Forms of . . . Government"—*Prose Works,* I, 206) did not survive the realignment of Swift's political allegiances in 1710. The portrait of Somers in *Four Last Years of the Queen* (discussed below) is an interesting exercise in corrective characterization. For further discussion of Swift's use of the antipanegyric in *Tale of a Tub,* see Miriam Starkman, *Swift's Satire on Learning in "A Tale of a Tub"* (Princeton, N. J., 1950).

They have in Ireland the same idea with Us, of Your Lordship's Generosity, Magnificence, Witt, Judgment, and Knowledge in the Enjoyment of Life. But I shall quickly undeceive them, by letting them plainly know, that you have neither Interest nor fortune which You can call your own; both having been long made over to the Corporation of deserving Men in Want. . . .*

Characterization by means of raillery (or, in reverse process, by means of mock-panegyric) was to serve Swift well throughout most of his career. However, when in 1710 he became a polemicist for the Harley–St. John ministry and faced the task of depicting the characters of his Tory friends and Whig enemies, he found it desirable to turn to different means. A technique so palpably ironic as raillery would have been out of keeping with Swift's pretensions as a historian. In the relatively informal pages of the *Examiner,* Swift could still offer an ironical list of the "defects" in the characters of the Tory ministers (*Examiner* 26), but in his more seriously intended tracts, such as *Four Last Years of the Queen,* he makes a point of promising that he will avoid mingling "Panegyrick or Satire with an History intended to inform Posterity . . . ," since personal bias, other than a normal love of virtue and hatred of vice, would be unbecoming in a man who sets himself up as a teller of truth. The proper attitude for a conscientious historian, Swift feels, is a sort of Olympian detachment from the men and events he describes, for "Facts truly related are the best Applauses, or most lasting Reproaches" (VII, 1–2). This is not to say that the historian should be morally neutral or indifferent, but merely that he should refrain from overtly imposing his emotional judgments upon the reader.

It is in terms of this ideal that Swift judges the Character of Charles II

* *The Correspondence of Jonathan Swift,* ed. Sir Harold Williams (Oxford, 1963–65), I, 143. Halifax, like Somers, was another of the Whig lords whose favor Swift unsuccessfully sought before 1710. Behind the surface irony of Swift's graceful compliment to him in this letter there lurks another irony of a more private kind; for despite his hopeful praise of Halifax' liberality toward "deserving Men," Swift's bitterness over his own neglected claims had been building up for some time. When, toward the end of his life, he came across a description of Halifax (in *Characters of the Court of Britain* by John Macky—1733) as "a great ENCOURAGER OF LEARNING and LEARNED MEN," Swift's terse marginal comment was: "His encouragements were onely good words and dinners—I never heard him say one good thing or seem to tast what was said by another" (*Prose Works,* V, 258).

in Bishop Burnet's *History of His Own Times* as "poorly drawn, and mingled with malice very unworthy [of] an historian . . ." (V, 283). Likewise, of his own portrayals of the members of the Whig Junto in *Four Last Years of the Queen,* Swift remarks (in *Enquiry into the Behaviour of the Queen's Last Ministry*—1715):

. . . I take this Opportunity of assuring those who may happen some Years hence to read the History I have written, that the blackest Characters to be met with in it, were not drawn with the least Mixture of Malice or ill Will; but meerly [*sic*] to expose the Odiousness of Vice; For I have always held it as a Maxim, that ill Men are placed beyond the Reach of an Historian, who indeed hath it in his Power to reward Virtue, but not to punish Vice. [VIII, 141]

Needless to say, in practice Swift is far from being as free of malice or ill will as he professes himself to be, and in fact, Olympian "detachment" functioned in his hands as a weapon infinitely more annihilating than an emotional attack would have been. In an age when any public figure could assume as a matter of course that he would be the target of innumerable bitterly personal assaults, Swift's "malice-free" portraits of the Whig lords in *Four Last Years of the Queen* were all the more telling for their indirection.

The "detachment" which Swift employs in describing the members of the Whig Junto has something in it of the manner appropriate to a zoologist describing a noxious animal. The analogy is one which Swift suggests himself, as in the *Short Character of Wharton* he explains that, "Whoever, for the Sake of others, were to describe the Nature of a Serpent, a Wolf, a Crocodile or a Fox, must be understood to do it without any personal Love or Hatred for the Animals themselves" (III, 178). Fifteen years later, in describing his attitude toward Walpole, Swift was to resort to similar terms. Writing to Pope on November 26, 1725, he remarks, "I am no more angry with [Walpole] than I was with the Kite that last week flew away with one of my Chickins and yet I was pleas'd when one of my Servants Shot him two days after. . . ."[3] Implied in these statements are the convenient assumptions that the vices of the men in question are (1) inherent, and (2) generally acknowledged. In such cases, the Character-writer can affect to act on the understanding that, like the zoologist describing a viper, he need not spend much time in arguing that the noxious quality actually exists and that it is evil. This is not to say that he will ignore it—indeed, it is his central topic—but merely that he will be free to turn his attention to an ostensibly dispassionate measurement of its precise dimensions.

Swift's first full-scale use of this approach was in the *Short Character of His Excellency Thomas Earl of Wharton,* written at the outset of his career as a Tory polemicist. Though in later years he was to describe Wharton as "The most universal Vilain I ever knew" (V, 259), in opening the *Short Character* Swift is careful to assure his readers that "his Excellency is one whom I neither personally love nor hate" (III, 178 ff.). Despite his professed detachment, Swift's loathing for Wharton is apparent in every line of the *Short Character,* but, as Swift's own analogy suggests, it is the cold loathing mixed with fascination to be expected in a man who undertakes to describe a repellent animal. "I never wonder to see Men wicked, but I often wonder to see them not ashamed" (IV, 251), Swift wrote in his *Thoughts on Various Subjects,* and this could well serve as the motto for his *Short Character of Wharton.*

"He is without the Sense of Shame or Glory, as some Men are without the Sense of Smelling . . . ," says Swift by way of preface, "So that I enter on the Work with more Chearfulness, because I am sure, neither to make him angry, nor [in] any Way hurt his Reputation; a Pitch of Happiness and Security to which his Excellency hath arrived, which no Philosopher before him could reach." Like his disclaimer of personal malice, Swift's insistence upon Wharton's presumed indifference to praise or blame is another element calculated to reinforce the zoologist pose. The lack of sensibility ascribed to Wharton is inhuman, and it helps to reduce him to the level of the serpent, wolf, crocodile, and fox to whom Swift has already compared him, for they too have natures which render them supremely indifferent to public opinion and moral exhortation. Swift strengthens the animal parallel as he goes on to describe Wharton's qualities. In almost every case, Swift makes the point, either explicitly or by implication, that Wharton's vices are so fundamental to his nature that they have become instinctive. Thus, although Wharton "hath some Years passed his Grand Climacteric" and occupies the dignified post of lieutenant governor, his conversation and manners continue to be those of a rambunctious youth, "and, all this is without Consequence, because it is in his Character, and what every Body expecteth." Likewise, Wharton's major trait—his love of lies and intrigue—is described as compulsive.

Many of his lies are gratuitous, for they are either unnecessary or such as can be "sometimes detected in an Hour, often in a Day, and always in a Week." Yet, so ingrained is the habit, that Wharton continues to tell lies even to men who he knows "will discover them the Moment they leave him." Clearly, to take a hortative tone toward such a creature would be without point, and as Swift goes on to describe Wharton's atheism, his profanity, his wenching, and his avarice, he carefully avoids expressing any emotion stronger than a sense of surprise at how easily Wharton has fooled the world.

When, three years later, Swift came to write the Characters of the Whig lords in *Four Last Years of the Queen,* he found that the icy detachment suitable for a Wharton could, with modifications, serve equally well as an approach to Wharton's colleagues. In general, Swift retains his zoologist's attitude, but unlike a zoologist, he now openly assumes the artist's prerogative of limiting himself to selective detail. Introducing his gallery of Whig notables, he says:

It may not be improper to describe those Qualities in Each of them, which few of their Admirers will deny, and which appear chiefly to have influenced them in acting their several Parts upon the publick Stage: For, I do not pretend to draw their Characters entire, which would be tedious, and little to the purpose; but shall only single out those Passions, Acquirements and Habits, which the Owners were most likely to transferr [*sic*] into their Political Schemes; and which were most subservient to the Designs they seemed to have in View. [VII, 5]

The advantages of such a policy are obvious: the decision as to what in each man's character may or may not be relevant is left solely to Swift's own discretion. Introducing the work in 1758, Dr. Charles Lucas felt obliged to ask rhetorically: "What writing, what sentence, what character can stand this torture?—What extreme perversion may not, let me say, does not, this produce?" (VII, 174). The reader's trust in the accuracy of such selective portraiture depends largely upon how far he accepts Swift's professions of good faith. Naturally, no Whigs (and, in 1758, only the most dedicated Tories) would be likely to accept at face value Swift's bold claim to disinterestedness. However, we may assume that the Tory squires and clergymen for whom Swift wrote the work in 1713 would have been generally predisposed to find the portraits both balanced and judicious.

The first of the Whigs whose Character Swift undertakes to give in *Four Last Years of the Queen* is Lord Somers. The task of pillorying the man whom he had ten years earlier eulogized in the dedication to *Tale of a Tub* was an especially delicate one. Many readers who were aware of Swift's identity could be expected to recall the earlier characterization, and a frontal attack upon Somers at this time would inevitably have suggested embarrassing comparisons. In such circumstances, Swift's pose of scientific detachment offered a particularly useful approach. The "Wit, and Eloquence, and Learning, and Wisdom, and Justice, and Politeness, and Candor, and Evenness of Temper" (I, 15) with which Swift had previously credited Somers did not have to be openly denied; instead they could merely be glossed over (as true, perhaps, but irrelevant) or, more effectively, they could be freely acknowledged and then diminished by subtle "explanations" and qualifications.

Swift begins the latter process at once, telling us that Somers "hath raised himself . . . to the greatest Employments of State, without the least Support from Birth or Fortune: He hath constantly, and with great Steadiness cultivated those Principles under which he grew" (VII, 5 ff.). The surface tone of these statements is factual and even laudatory, but an element of ambiguity is introduced by the reference to Somers' modest origins. Not many Tory readers would be inclined to admire either self-made men or the principles, however steadily cultivated, which such a background might be expected to foster. The point is repeated a few lines later, this time more explicitly, when Swift explains that after the Revolution, "the old Republican Spirit" led Whig politicians to seek protégés who were "perfectly indifferent to any or no Religion; and, who were not likely to inherit much Loyalty from those to whom they owed their Birth. Of this Number was the Person I am now describing." As if to counterbalance so direct a criticism, Swift next makes what seems at first a generous compliment, saying: "I have hardly known any man with Talents more proper to acquire and preserve the Favour of a Prince; never offending in Word or Gesture, which are in the highest degree Courteous and Complaisant." This "extreme Civility," however, is not universally admired, for "it is sometimes censured as formal."

With this last phrase, we see Swift turning to the vague ascription—one of the devices he found most useful in his role of detached observer. In this technique, Swift introduces criticism of his victims either by way of the passive voice ("it has been said that he is . . .") or by citing unspecified sources ("some people say that he is . . ."). Such methods for gaining the effect of slander without taking on the responsibility for it are, of course, nothing new, but Swift puts them to particularly effective use; for his vaguely ascribed charges are almost invariably introduced in order to give him the opportunity, in his role as judicious weigher of evidence, to bring up some damaging "defense" or "explanation" on behalf of the victim. Thus, to those who complain that Lord Somers' evenness of demeanor is overly formal, Swift answers (1) that Somers, being conscious of his lowly origins, is suspicious of all familiarity; and (2) his temper is by nature so given to violent passions that he dare not incite it by even the slightest surrender to emotion. Swift resorts again to the passive voice in describing how Somers' "Breast hath been seen to heave, and his Eyes to sparkle with Rage, in those very moments when his Words and the Cadence of his Voice were in the humblest and softest manner." This violence of temper, Swift muses, may likewise be responsible for "that insatiable Love of Revenge" with which "his Detractors" charge Somers. In the remainder of the Character, Swift grants Somers his virtues, but somehow those which do not turn out to be purely negative—e.g., "Avarice he hath none"—seem mostly to be vices in disguise.

The same basic techniques are applied, in varying degrees, to the seven other Whig notables whose Characters follow Somers' in *Four Last Years of the Queen*. Almost every subject is the victim of anonymous "Maligners," who make damaging accusations against him, and of equally anonymous "Admirers," who credit him with dubious virtues. Like a man carefully weighing evidence, Swift unemotionally considers each point and offers his opinion, only rarely allowing any signs of overt rancor to show through his careful façade of detachment. Even the most extreme charges are delivered obliquely and in the manner of one who wishes to be scrupulously fair, as is the case, for example, when Swift assures his readers that it was merely love of money which led the Duke of Marlborough to seek a lifetime generalship, for "I am persuaded . . . that he had *then* no Intentions of settling the Crown in his Family; his only Son having been dead some years before" (VII, 7).

Elsewhere in his tracts, especially those in which he makes no real claim to the title of historian, Swift may resort to methods of hostile characterization more direct than these. His attack on Steele in the *Importance of the "Guardian" Considered,* for example, is a more or less straightforward frontal assault in which there is little pretense of detachment beyond the perfunctory opening remark, "I owe him no Malice" (VIII, 5). Likewise, when dealing with foreigners, Swift has only to turn to one of the unflattering national stereotypes of outsiders with which England has always been well supplied. In this manner, ready-made Characters, as it were, are available for the French Guiscard (he is erratic and prone to impulsive violence—III, 107–8); for the Dutch M. Buys (he is dull and grasping—VII, 23); and for the Italian Prince Eugene (he is vain and cruel—VII, 26). On the whole, however, Swift found that the pose of detachment, as exemplified in the *Short Character of Wharton* and the Whig portraits which open *Four Last Years of the Queen,* was the method of characterization best suited to his role as a writer of history.

Swift seldom cares to relinquish the offensive in his political tracts, and accordingly his friendly portraits of Tory heroes are far fewer in number than his hostile ones of Whig villains. As opposed to his rogue's gallery of eight Whig ministers at the beginning of *Four Last Years of the Queen,* Swift offers a formal Character of only one Tory minister—the treasurer, Robert Harley. Swift is careful not to place his portrait of Harley in juxtaposition to those of the Whig leaders, for to do so would be to risk making his bias unavoidably obvious. The work, therefore, is well along before Swift interrupts his narrative to describe Harley. In portraying his friend, Swift employs much the same pretense of detachment he has used toward the Whig leaders, though the detachment now has been transformed into a vehicle of praise rather than of attack. After opening with references to Harley's "Wisdom and Fidelity," Swift admits that he is uncommonly secretive, but only because experience has shown him "That a Secret is seldom Safe in more than One Breast" (VII, 73 ff.). In like manner, throughout the Character Swift makes no real attempt to deny Harley's weaknesses, though most of the defects he attributes to his subject are minor and easily forgivable. When, as is sometimes the case, they are of a more serious nature, Swift makes sure to see that each vice is coupled with a long list of virtues ("Fear, Avarice, Cruelty, and Pride are wholly strangers to his Nature; but he is not without Ambition").

As he had done in his Whig portraits, Swift leans heavily upon vague ascription. Thus, Harley's "Detractours" charge him with cunning. "He hath been blamed by his Friends" for not seeking outside advice; and "Some have censured him" as being jealous of his power. Conceding that Harley occasionally gives the appearance of such vices, Swift nevertheless insists that in reality he is guilty of none of them. The false impression arises from his love of secrecy, which, though Swift clearly labels it a defect, has been shown to be both understandable and excusable in a man burdened with such great responsibilities. At one point, Swift displays his detachment by volunteering a new charge of his own against Harley, saying:

There is One Thing peculiar in his Temper, which I altogether disapprove . . . ; I mean an Easiness and Indifference under any Imputation, although he be ever so Innocent. . . . So that I have known him often suspected by his nearest Friends . . . to a degree that they were ready to break with him, and only undeceived by Time or Accident. [VII, 74]

Though Swift speaks of such equanimity in the face of attack as a quality which he does not "remember to have heard or met with in any other Man's Character," it will be recalled that the Earl of Wharton was likewise a man whom Swift found undisturbed by reflections upon his name. Swift affects to disapprove of this trait in Harley, but in describing it, he makes it clear that Harley's indifference to attack springs from an awareness of his own virtue. The same quality in Wharton, as Swift had pictured it, reflected nothing more than Wharton's well-justified conviction that his reputation was already sunk so low as to be immune to either flattery or slander.

As a means of praise, Swift's pose of detachment is rather less successful than it had been when used, as originally designed, for attack. Had his pose as a historian allowed it, Swift would doubtless have chosen to issue his praise in the form of raillery,[4] and, in fact, there are elements of raillery in the way he "criticizes" Harley for insignificant or unreal defects. It is in the nature of things that vice and weakness are more easily made believable than are virtue and strength, and in this portrait of Harley, the foibles described (although minor) tend to stick in the mind in a way that his considerable virtues do not. The detachment which gave Swift's hostile Characters a tone of ostensible impartiality, lends this friendly Character a defensive quality, and Swift, as if sensing this, generally reserves his pose of detachment for the description of Whig enemies.

There are exceptions to this rule, however, such as the Characters of Harley and St. John which appear in the *Enquiry Into the Behaviour of the Queen's Last Ministry* (1715). This work, written in Ireland after the fall of the Tory ministry, was not intended for general publication, and accordingly, it is more of a private record than a polemical tract. Though he is naturally interested in justifying the late ministry and his role in it, Swift is here more immediately concerned with an honest attempt to discover the reasons behind the Tory downfall. The detachment with which he views Harley and St. John in this work is, given Swift's affection and respect for both men, far more real than the pseudo detachment he applies to characterization in his more public writings. Swift, relieved of the necessity of functioning primarily as a propagandist, is now able to concede real faults in his friends. He need no longer suppress or offer excuses for Harley's morbid suspiciousness and his ruinous procrastination; nor need he any longer ignore St. John's vanity and his rakishness. Inevitably, Swift finds much more good than bad to say about the two men, and both portraits are overwhelmingly favorable. Nevertheless, had Swift been writing for public consumption, it is unlikely that he would have been willing to discuss what displeased him about his two friends in such a genuinely detached manner.*

For his public tracts, Swift never found a means of favorable characterization altogether suitable to his purposes. Detachment, whether real or assumed, had a way of making praise sound lukewarm. Raillery, on the other hand, was out of keeping with his pose as a historian, and the same was true of open panegyric. Swift solved his problem to some extent simply by avoiding it, for, as was noted earlier, formal Characters of his

---

* There are analogous cases in the few brief Characters of personal acquaintances which have survived among Swift's papers. These sketches, which were usually occasioned by the person's death, include studies of Primate Marsh, of Stella, of Mrs. Howard, and of Dr. Sheridan. None of these Characters, with the possible exception of Mrs. Howard's, were intended for publication, and accordingly, Swift foregoes most of his usual polemical techniques and merely sets down his private opinions on a take-it-or-leave-it basis. Only the adored Stella receives a eulogy—the faults and virtues of the others are subjected to a direct and unsentimental analysis designed for descriptive, rather than persuasive, ends.

political allies are relatively few in Swift's Tory tracts. Such avoidance, in any case, was desirable, since it was much to Swift's polemical advantage to picture the Tory campaign for peace as one waged on a plane superior to petty personalities—in contrast to the Whig cause, with its domination by a group of power-hungry politicians.* With a few exceptions like those noted, Swift prefers to deliver his praise of individuals in the form of short descriptive asides, rather than in full-dress character sketches. In this way, Swift can pay his compliments in relatively unobtrusive fashion, thus avoiding the sort of unseemly eulogy which would be out of place in a history. Accordingly, in the *Four Last Years of the Queen,* St. John (twenty-five pages after the lengthy "detached" portrait of Harley) is briefly summed up as a man possessed "of an extraordinary Genius, and Application to Publick Affairs, joined with an invincible Eloquence" (VII, 98). Though some such flattering description is applied to each Tory notable as he makes his first appearance in the narrative, Swift is usually careful not to make these passing compliments (except those to the queen) either long enough or extravagant enough to invite skepticism.

Writing in *Examiner* 34, Swift had once complained of how his strictly truthful descriptions of Whig and Tory leaders were misread by hostile readers as wildly exaggerated satires or panegyrics. Such confusion, he felt, was perhaps understandable, for "suppose I should write the Character of an Honest, a Religious, and a learned Man, and send the first to *Newgate,* and the second to the *Grecian Coffee-House,* and the last to *White's;* would they not all pass for *Satyrs,* and justly enough, among the Companies to whom they were sent?" (III, 119). Behind the irony of this complaint lies Swift's awareness of the skepticism certain to be encountered by anyone who, like himself, claims to write with impartiality of current politics and political figures. A pretense to detachment is all but universal among writers upon political subjects, and in fact, one of the

* In this connection, Swift's descriptive references to the queen form a special category of their own, for she is the one person with whom Swift is actually very anxious to associate the Tory cause. As the title of his most ambitious tract indicates, Swift wanted his readers to think of Anne as his protagonist and, in fact, as the personification of the Tory party. Swift nowhere gives a formal Character of the queen, but both convention and expedience dictated that he offer her frequent and fulsome praise. Accordingly, he shows no hesitation in directing toward her the sort of unrestrained panegyrics he elsewhere avoids.

signs by which we recognize the polemicist is the frequency with which he protests his lack of prejudice. As we have seen, Swift supports his own claim to detachment (particularly in his longer Tory tracts), by affecting the manner of an impartial historian—or, to use one of his favorite metaphors, of a surgeon impersonally dissecting a body. When Swift puts on his figurative surgeon's smock in the political tracts, he does not, except in the loosest sense, assume a persona; the "detachment" displayed is meant to be accepted as genuine and as Swift's own. Accordingly, in works like the *Four Last Years of the Queen,* he avoids any overt satire which might tend to violate the dignity of his scientific dispassion. Outside his political tracts, however, free of his self-imposed ban on satire, Swift knew that the pose which had served him so well as a serious weapon could function no less effectively when used for satiric purposes. All that was necessary was that he take on a deliberate persona in the form of some self-deceived enthusiast—a Gulliver or the projector of the *Modest Proposal*—whose solemn professions of detachment were so transparently false or meaningless that the reader, in discounting them, could be expected to lean toward acceptance of Swift's underlying satiric message. My discussion of these techniques has been focused primarily upon their use in the portrayal of character, but much of what has been pointed out in this connection may also be applied to Swift's more general polemical practice in both the relatively straightforward Tory tracts and the more complex satiric works upon which his reputation has always found its most solid basis.

Six: Swift and Defoe

If so exalted a title could properly be applied to a subject so essentially mundane, one might call the reign of Queen Anne "the Golden Age of British Political Pamphleteering." Never before or after did so many prominent literary figures devote so much skill and passion to undisguised political controversy. The resultant corpus of tracts, periodicals, broadsheets, and pamphlets is of an imposing size. Of the thirteen volumes in Swift's collected *Prose Works,* the Tory tracts fill four (III, VI, VII, VIII)—almost a third of his total work in prose. Defoe's *Review* alone fills twenty-two sizable volumes in a facsimile edition,[1] to which may be added such works as the massive *History of the Union Between England and Scotland* and the numerous individual tracts ascribed to him—all written during the 1704–14 period. If we add to these the party tracts of such men as Steele and Prior, who regularly engaged in political pamphleteering, and further include the mass of material furnished by the countless anonymous or half-forgotten Grub Street hacks who formed the bulk of the party press, we can see that it would take a respectably large bookcase to house the surviving Whig and Tory polemics of Queen Anne's brief but crowded reign.

Even a casual survey of so large a mass of material, while interesting in itself, would be beyond the scope of the present study. Nevertheless, it is desirable in considering Swift's political tracts to attempt to place those tracts within the context of contemporary pamphleteering. Accordingly, in this chapter it is my intention briefly to compare Swift's role as a propagandist with that of his most notable rival, Daniel Defoe. Not only was Defoe among the most prolific and (along with Swift) the most accomplished propagandists of the Augustan Age, but the basic divergencies and the occasional curious parallels between the two men's works

93

seem to invite a comparison. More specifically, I wish to focus upon Swift and Defoe in terms of their respective audiences and to show that many of the conspicuous differences between these two apologists for the Harley administration can be best explained by reference to the differences between what each man's readers required.

The general nature of the relationship between Swift and Defoe has been the subject of a full-length study by John F. Ross,[2] though his primary concern has been not with either man's political tracts, but rather with the resemblances and dissimilarities of their respective masterpieces, *Gulliver's Travels* and *Robinson Crusoe*. Ross has examined the works of each man in search of references to the other, and as we read the list of such references, we become aware of a mutual, though curiously lopsided, antagonism. There is no evidence to indicate that the two authors ever met, though both, in the 1710–14 period, were closely involved with Harley—Swift as a proud friend, and Defoe as a furtive employee. As early as 1705, in the *Consolidator,* Defoe had made slighting reference to the *"Blasphemy"* of the *Tale of a Tub,* and his remark that the author "took Shipping to *Dublin"* shows he was aware of Swift's identity. In 1708, writing against the repeal of the Sacramental Test in Ireland, Swift (still an ostensible Whig) took the opportunity to denounce the "weekly Libellers" who opposed the Test, commenting: "One of these Authors (the Fellow that was *pilloryed,* I have forgot his Name) is indeed so grave, sententious, dogmatical a Rogue, that there is no enduring him." [3] Such were the initial references of each man to the other.

By 1710, when he had assumed the editorship of the *Examiner,* Swift found a second occasion to refer to Defoe. Surveying rival pamphleteers, Swift remarks that on the Whig side there are

. . . two stupid illiterate Scribblers, both of them *Fanaticks* by Profession; I mean the *Review* and *Observator.* . . . I cannot but suspect, that [these] two *Worthies* . . . have in a Degree done Mischief among us; the mock authoritative Manner of the one, and the insipid Mirth of the other, however insupportable to reasonable Ears, being of a Level with great Numbers among the lowest Part of Mankind. [*Prose Works,* III, 13–14]

This was Swift's final direct reference to Defoe. Thereafter he ignored both the man and his works, either feeling or affecting to feel that they were beneath his notice. But Defoe, who had ignored Swift's earlier barb, was now goaded into a disproportionately prolonged and vehement reply.

In the *Review* for December 14, 1710, after first announcing that the only appropriate answer to such abuse is disdainful silence, Defoe nevertheless proceeds to devote most of the issue and much of the next as well (December 16, 1710) to an attack upon the *Examiner* as a boor and libeler. Defoe's reply may be summarized as follows: the *Examiner* calls me stupid and illiterate, yet if he really believes me so, why does he bother to notice me at all? "When a Man calls another Fool, Stupid, Ideot, Illiterate, &c. and then pretends to enter Debate with him—'Tis absurd." Since the *Examiner* seems to pride himself so much upon his "Learning," how is it he has such ill manners as to attack someone he has already dismissed as his intellectual and social inferior? A gentleman should be "angry like a Gentleman," and the *Examiner,* by resorting to "Billingsgate" in attacking me, clearly demonstrates that it is he, rather than myself, who is ill bred. As for the charge that I am an "Ideot" and "unlearned"—there is a man I could name who is a prodigy of learning, "but at the same time, he is a *Cynick* in Behaviour, a *Fury* in Temper, *Unpolite* in Conversation, *Abusive* and *Scurrilous* in Language, and *Ungovernable* in Passion—Is this to be Learned? Then *may I be still Illiterate.*" In any case, I am the master of five languages, have read Euclid's *Elements,* have gone "some length in Physicks, or Natural Philosophy, . . . thought myself Master of Geography," and am skilled in almanac making and astronomy. Therefore, I am content to let the world judge the truth of Mr. *Examiner*'s charges.

It is interesting to note that Defoe seems to have been most stung by the words "stupid" and "illiterate" (applied by Swift to both the *Review* and the *Observator*), rather than by the slurring reference to his "mock authoritative Manner." It is likewise interesting that into Swift's brief and rather perfunctory attack, Defoe reads a whole range of insults not apparent on the surface. Swift, perhaps heeding Defoe's advice, ignored this attack upon himself, as well as the subsequent ones Defoe was periodically to make in the *Review* and elsewhere.

I have treated at some length this exchange of insults between the two men because the nature of Swift's charges and the character of Defoe's reply and countercharges cast light upon each man's public character as a pamphleteer, and by implication, upon his audience and techniques. It will be noticed that Swift's few references to Defoe are brief, cool, and casually disdainful. It may be doubted whether Swift, as an accomplished polemicist, really had so low an opinion of Defoe's abilities, but in his public references to Defoe, at any rate, his tone appears to be one of authentic contempt. Though Defoe suggests that Swift has stooped to vulgar mudslinging unbecoming a gentleman, in fact it is precisely the "gentlemanliness" of the attack which Defoe finds most offensive. To have been scurrilously denounced as a liar and a rogue would have been no more than Defoe was used to; but to be so casually dismissed as a fatuous, low fellow, whose very name it was below the dignity of a gentleman to remember, was intolerable. Defoe, quite correctly, interprets Swift's contempt as springing largely from social, rather than merely political, sources, and he chooses to answer it in social and personal terms. As a Dissenter and a representative of tradesmen, Defoe stood for everything Swift found most threatening to the social order he valued, but Swift wisely refrains from engaging in anything so unseemly as the exchange of abuse which Defoe's long countercharges invite (though when a gentleman, such as Steele, is the adversary, Swift is not above such an exchange).[4]

It will be further noticed that not only is Defoe's reply to Swift disproportionately long, but he also magnifies what Swift has said, even going so far as to place words like "Ideot" and "Fool" in his mouth. Defoe's querulous tone and the undignified cataloguing of his own learning suggest the fury of a man who has digested one too many casual snubs from those whose social positions make them his automatic and inevitable superiors. To Defoe—aware of his own abilities, conscious of his important service to Harley, and belligerently proud of his tradesman background—it must have been a bitter experience to see Swift honored and flattered as Harley's intimate and equal while he was limited (albeit voluntarily) to secret meetings and reduced to plaintive letters petitioning for money. Moreover, the resentment Defoe felt over Swift's easy assumption of superiority would find an immediate response in most of his readers. Just as Swift's country squire readership would have considered his tone toward Defoe as altogether appropriate, so must the urban tradesmen who formed the *Review*'s primary audience have found Defoe's defense a proper rebuttal.

That Defoe wrote the *Review* and his other pamphlets with primarily an urban commercial audience in mind is demonstrated on almost every page of his political writings. Although, like any good rhetor, Defoe occasionally protests that he writes for all honest patriots, rather than for any special group or class, the specific nature of his audience is clearly indicated by his subject matter and his appeals. The *Review,* on its first appearance in 1704, offered readers *A Weekly Review of the Affairs of France, Purg'd from the Errors and Partiality of News-Writers and Petty-Statesmen, of all Sides.* However, instead of the political and historical approach which such a title would seem to promise, readers of the *Review* from the first were given a heavy diet of essays concerned with the importance of trade and commerce in British life. Even the story of the wars with France—the paper's ostensible focus of interest—quickly became secondary to such matters as the forthcoming union with Scotland and the beneficial effects that would result in Britain's economic life.

The nature of Defoe's subject matter eventually led to changes in the title of the periodical. With the appearance of Volume II, the earlier title had been shortened and modified to *A Review of the Affairs of FRANCE: With Some Observations on Transactions at Home.* By Volume III, this had been further changed to *A Review of the State of the English Nation*—reivsed in Volume IV, after the union with Scotland, to *A Review of the State of the British Nation.* This title then remained in use until Volume IX, when the one word, *Review,* was substituted. In the preface to the first collected volume of the *Review* (1705) Defoe apologizes to his readers for "bringing the Story of *France* down to the matter of Trade," confessing that by doing so he has entered "a vast Wilderness of a Subject, so large, that I know not where it will end." Yet, he says, he will continue to explore this wilderness, for he believes

. . . that the matter of our *English* Trade appears to be a thing of such Consequence to be treated of, so much pretended to, and so little understood, that nothing could be more profitable to the Readers, more advantageous to the publick Interest of this Nation, or more suitable to the Greatness of this Undertaking, than to make an Essay at the Evils, Causes, and Remedies of our general *Negoce* [*sic*].[5]

Defoe was as good as his word, for in the following eight years he wrote of no subject with greater regularity and enthusiasm than "the most delightful as well as profitable Subject of the *English* Trade."

The sort of audience toward which this was directed is at least partly indicated in a statement by Charles Leslie, the editor of the High-Tory *Rehearsal,* who started his own paper, he says, in order to counteract the evil influence of Defoe's *Review.* The public of the *Review,* Leslie tells us, is largely urban and illiterate, and they absorb the paper's arguments by gathering "together about one that can read and listen . . . (as I have seen them in the streets)." [6] Likewise, Ned Ward, in his *Vulgus Britannicus,* describes the *Review* and *Observator* as "the two Good Old Cause asserters, / Read most by cobblers and by porters." [7]

It is illustrative of the ambiguity of Defoe's role and of party designations in Queen Anne's time that Ward links the ostensibly neutral *Review* with the vehemently Whig *Observator,* whose editor, John Tutchin, was literally beaten to death in 1707—at the hands, as was plausibly believed at the time, of outraged Tories. Swift, in his comment quoted earlier, likewise automatically categorizes the *Review* along with the *Observator* as a Whig paper, though in fact Defoe was subsidized by Harley and, despite token criticism and reservations, regularly backed his policies. To the modern American reader, acquainted with a system wherein each party harbors men whose political philosophies are widely divergent, it should not seem odd that two men arguing for the same ministry should yet consider themselves political opponents. As I have suggested, a good deal of the basic cleavage between Swift and Defoe (and, by extension, between Tory and Whig) was social, religious, and economic, rather than solely political. Though Swift's and Defoe's stated political objectives might be much the same, the differences between their audiences and the terms in which these audiences might be reached justified the hostility with which the two men faced each other.

It would be a mistake, however, to assume that Defoe's audience was primarily composed of cobblers and porters. Both Leslie and Ward, like Swift, were fervent Tories to whom *any* tradesman, however middle class, was apt to appear as an illiterate cobbler with social pretensions—a figure either ludicrous or dangerous, depending upon how much economic power he and his fellows wielded. The working class, as we know it today, scarcely existed in the early eighteenth century, and the servant class, though sizable, was without formal political power. The franchise extended only to those who had property or land to the value of forty shillings or more, and the urban working population, such as it was, had no significant political voice except in its intermittent role as the "Mob," feared almost equally by Whig and Tory alike. Though porters and the like might read the *Review* or have it read to them, Defoe was not so naïve as to waste his efforts (nor Harley his money) upon so peripheral a group.

Defoe's real audience was the commercial middle class which had developed since the Restoration. At one end were the small, independent tradesmen—shopkeepers, entrepreneurs, and craftsmen—and at the other end were the well-to-do, often enormously wealthy, dealers in wholesale goods, shipowners, and investors in such commercial enterprises as the Hudson's Bay Company. This audience, though at its upper levels it might encompass a good many members of the gentry, was in general terms the "Mony'd Interest" which Swift so scorned and which, as he realized, was seriously challenging the power of the landowning gentry for whom the *Examiner, Conduct of the Allies,* and *Four Last Years of the Queen* were written. As a moderate politician, Harley naturally sought support from both groups, and if Swift's task was to convince the rural squires that the Harley–St. John ministry would guard their interests, Defoe's rather more difficult task was to convince the urban commercial classes that the Tories would be equally solicitous on their behalf. That Defoe had no intention of addressing the same audience Swift spoke to may be seen by the nature of his remarks concerning the landowning class. In the index to the facsimile edition of the *Review,* the group of such references reads: "GENTRY . . . trade enriches, II, 10a; despise trade families, III, 6b; dishonor of, 29b; . . . scorn public service, learning, V, 403a; riches of, effeminates spirit, 406a; . . . idle are drones, VI, 135a; . . . example of, encourages vice, 255a;" and so on.[8]

In addressing his audience of rural gentry, Swift, as we have seen, generally assumed no elaborate fictional persona, but rather offered his own character in somewhat idealized form as an accurate reflection of the country squire as he viewed himself—reasonable, staunchly patriotic, and dedicated to queen and Church. Defoe, to an even greater extent than Swift, dispenses with any mask between himself and his readers. So completely does Defoe give himself to his audience that if nothing of his writings had survived save the *Review,* a fairly detailed biography could be written of his life to 1713 on the basis of that work alone. From the first, Defoe's identity as the author of the *Review* was widely suspected, and he soon removed all doubts, as with increasing frequency he offered autobiographical details about such matters as his imprisonment over the *Shortest Way With Dissenters,* his successes and failures in business, his money difficulties, his education, and his family problems. The thinness of Defoe's pretense to anonymity may be seen in the *Review* of 1708, wherein Defoe tells of being introduced to a gentleman who, upon hearing his name, says, "Who[,] *D. F.* . . . , the Author of the *True-Born-Englishman?* Yes Sir quo[th] I . . . , very mannerly—What[,] says he again, the same Man that writes the *Review?* The same[,] Sir, quo[th] I again" (*Review,* V, 147). By August 5, 1710, Defoe has given up even such feeble attempts at concealment, and he prints his name in full as author.

In revealing so much of himself to his readers and in making his personal life a subject of discussion, Defoe is doing something rare in English journalism before this time—he is deliberately exploiting his own personality for rhetorical effect. This, as we shall see, creates a closeness of relationship between him and his audience that markedly differs from that between Swift and his readers. Though Swift may, as in the preface to *Four Last Years of the Queen,* give details of his personal life by way of supporting his claim to independence, he does not, as Defoe does regularly, offer gratuitous information concerning his private affairs. Swift always maintains a certain distance and reserve proper to a gentleman. In general, Swift's manner is that of a minister addressing his flock from a pulpit; Defoe's manner, on the other hand, is that of a garrulous and gossipy lay preacher risen at a meeting to cajole and twit his friends into righteousness. "Now *Protestants! Britains! English-Men!* or whatever I may call you, to win your Attention," Defoe typically addresses his audience in one *Review,* "will you once listen to a Contemptible Author, whom you have formerly allow'd to speak Sense, and grant me to be speaking for your Good, *this once,* if you never read what I write more?" (*Review,* VIII, 611).

The contrast in manner between Swift and Defoe is indicative of the differing assumptions of their respective audiences concerning what properly qualifies a man to function as a political journalist. Insofar as Swift finds it necessary to present his credentials to his readers, he suggests that it is his position as a friend to the great and as a privileged observer of secret affairs that gives him a claim to attention. In his earlier tracts, however, before his identity as author was generally known, Swift operates on a basic, though unexpressed, understanding with his audience that it is his status as a gentleman (with all that this implies in the way of education and social background), that entitles him to a hearing. Swift professes to find Defoe ludicrous not merely because of what he says, but largely because of what he is. It will be remembered that of Swift's two references to Defoe (cited earlier), one singles out for comment his "grave, sententious, dogmatical" manner and the other his "mock authoritative" tone. Swift seems to view Defoe much as he views the *"Fanatick Farmer"* and the footman whom he describes in *Examiner* 15 as engaging in abstruse theological dispute; from sources such as these, any pretense to seriousness is necessarily "sententious" and "mock authoritative." Defoe, on the other hand, proceeds on the assumption that his native wit and practical experience entitle him to a hearing and that matters of formal education and social background are irrelevant as qualifications. Though Defoe's steady intrusion of his private life into the *Review* might be destructive of dignity, providing such information was perhaps the most effective way of winning the confidence of an audience composed largely of self-made London tradesmen. A squire might respond with raised eyebrows to a man who publicly discussed the details of his personal history; to a shopkeeper, however, such discussion would seem altogether appropriate from a man who presumed to tell others what their politics should be.

But another, and perhaps more important, reason for Defoe's emphasis upon his own personality in the *Review* is tied in with the fact that Defoe's audience expected to be entertained as well as instructed. Originally each essay in the *Review* was followed by a brief *"Mercure Scandale; or Advice from the Scandalous Club,"* a social commentary designed, as Defoe tells his readers, to "Present you with a little Diversion, as any thing occurs to make the World Merry" (*Review,* I, 4). After Volume III, this feature was replaced by the "Miscellanea," more serious in tone than the "Advice," but still designed to attract readers who might not be receptive to an exclusively political paper. Nor did Defoe limit himself only to political matters in his main essays. Unlike Swift, who concentrates on party concerns, Defoe offers his opinions upon whatever he feels will strike his audience as timely. Thus, for example, *Review* VIII, 32, is devoted to a discussion of the avoidance and treatment of smallpox, and *Review* VIII, 90, deals with witchcraft and its dangers.

Defoe's readiness to express his ideas on any topic, however irrelevant to politics, which might interest his readers is in a sense merely another aspect of his exploitation of his personality. In effect, Defoe offers himself as a created character with whom the readers of the *Review* can identify themselves, and in whom they can feel a personal interest. The audience is tacitly invited to consider him as it would a friend—a friend whose history and idiosyncrasies are known, and to whose character and opinions, as they are gradually unfolded in the *Review,* there is attached a certain personal curiosity and even suspense.

In keeping with the nature of his audience and his rapport with it, Defoe eschews any elegance of style or elaborate literary embellishment. To some extent, of course, the plainness of Defoe's style in the *Review* results less from choice than from the conditions under which he wrote. For nine years Defoe unfailingly met his deadlines, though he was frequently obliged to write while traveling or otherwise engaged in Harley's business. The essays in the *Review* frequently show signs of haste, and it is not unusual to encounter whole paragraphs which, in their looseness of syntax and rambling construction, can barely be understood. But while Defoe may sometimes have been slapdash from necessity, the general informality of his style, with its conversational tone, its frequent digressions, and its unpretentious air, is the result of a deliberate effort to write in the manner best suited to reach his middle-class audience. When Defoe answers critics of his inelegant style, he offers two sorts of explanation. In the first sort, displaying a clear awareness of the nature of his audience, he defends himself by saying:

I could give you Similies, and Allegories to represent the Case to you, and read you long Lectures upon the *Roman* Affairs under the Government of their Counsuls and Tribunes. . . . But I have chosen a down-right Plainness, and to speak home both in Fact and in Stile: A Method however less safe to my self, yet more generally Instructing and Clear to the Understanding of the People I am speaking to. [*Review,* VII, 149]

In his second and more frequent variety of explanation for his plainness of expression, Defoe drops any hint of apology and proceeds to justify his style in terms of subject matter, rather than audience.

Let not those Gentlemen who are Criticks in Stile, in Method or Manner, be angry that I have never pull'd off my Cap to them in humble Excuse for my loose Way of treating the World as to Language, Expression, and Politeness of Phrase; . . . When I am busied writing Essays, and Matters of Science, I shall address them for their Aid, and take as much Care to avoid their Displeasure as becomes me; but when I am upon the Subject of Trade, and the Variety of Casual Story, I think my self a little loose from the Bonds of Cadence and Perfections of Stile, and satisfie my self in my Study to be explicit, easie, free, and very plain; and for all the rest, *Nec Careo, nec Curo.* [*Review,* I, iii–iv]

In both cases the appeal is to decorum; for just as Swift shrewdly judged what imagery, vocabulary, and allusion would best serve him with his audience of rural gentry, so Defoe sensed that a certain informality, even to the point of carelessness, would suit both his readers and his subject best.

In terms of rhetorical approach, perhaps the most important factor in dictating Defoe's techniques was the knowledge that his audience, unlike Swift's, was basically hostile to the Tories. Swift's country squires might have fears about the Pretender or reservations over a possibly dishonorable peace, but their instinctive sympathies lay with the Tory ministry, and Swift's task in defending that ministry was made simpler by the extent to which his audience was willing and even eager to be convinced. Defoe, however, in defending the same ministry, was facing an actively skeptical audience—one that was as emotionally committed to the Whig cause as Swift's was to the Tory. Clearly, Defoe could not address such an audience in the partisan tones Swift used; had he done so he would have merely aroused their immediate antagonism. In order to win a hearing, Defoe had first to cajole his readers into a receptive mood—hence, his "openness" about his personal life, his frequent inclusion of nonpolitical matters of general interest, and his use of an appropriately down-to-earth style. Like Swift, Defoe presents himself as a political moderate arguing a middle course between extremes; but while Swift is "moderate" only in terms of his already partisan audience, both personal inclination and the imperatives of his position lead Defoe to assume a more genuinely median stance.

An interesting example of the different approaches employed by the two men can be seen in their respective responses to the furor created by the Tories' dismissal of the Duke of Marlborough as general of the Allied armies. As has been mentioned elsewhere in this study, Marlborough, though his greatest popularity had passed, was still an idol to the Whigs, and even among many Tories he retained something of his earlier aura of heroism. Each man in this case was faced by the same task—to demonstrate the justice of Marlborough's removal and thus to stifle the public misgivings aroused by the Whig charges of national ingratitude. Swift discusses Marlborough's downfall briefly in several places, and of these I have chosen *Examiner* numbers 16 and 27 as representative of his treatment of the subject. The *Journal to Stella* reveals that Swift had considerable personal doubts over the wisdom of replacing so successful a general; for the purposes of the *Examiner,* however, he shows little sense of apprehension.

In opening *Examiner* 16, Swift acknowledges the delicacy of his subject, but craves his audience's indulgence, for, he says, "if I deliver my Sentiments with some Freedom, I hope it will be forgiven, while I accompany it with that Tenderness which so nice a Point requires" (*Prose Works,* III, 19 ff.). The "common Clamour of Tongues and Pens," he tells us, has for some time complained over the ingratitude shown to the Duke of Marlborough "in return of the most eminent Services that ever were performed by a Subject to his Country; not to be equalled in History." By ascribing such extravagant phraseology to the duke's supporters, Swift naturally invites the reader to consider if Marlborough's services have indeed been so great as advertised. A stranger to the fact, hearing the uproar, Swift goes on, might imagine that Marlborough had been executed, left to starve, or exiled. Yet, none of these things has been done. Instead, Marlborough, after a career full of financial rewards and official honors, has merely been relieved of his command. This being so, "Will the Accusers of the Nation . . . tell us in what Point our damnable Sin of Ingratitude lies?" Swift turns Marlborough's very popularity against him as he goes on to point out that "this is not an Age to produce Favourites of the People, while we live under a Queen who engrosseth all our Love, and all our Veneration"—the implication being that those who honor Marlborough do so only at the queen's expense. Further, it is remarkable, says Swift, that in a "detracting Age," the duke has for so long been spared any mention of "his *real Defects* (as nothing Human is without them)." Swift does not at this point specify what such defects might be, though they are hinted at when he next, after a long list of the tangible rewards the duke has received, remarks that "all this is but a

Trifle, in Comparison of what is *untold*." What follows next are the celebrated "Bill of *ROMAN* Gratitude" and "Bill of *BRITISH* Ingrati-tude"—discussed earlier in another connection—in which a Roman gen-eral's rewards ("A Crown of Laurel"—2*d.*) are contrasted with Marl-borough's ("Blenheim"—£200,000).

A few weeks later, in *Examiner* 27, Swift follows up this attack with a more personal assault. He opens with a few general observations on the evils of avarice, which, he points out, is at best a disfiguring vice in a private individual, but which becomes a dangerous one when found in a public figure, "such as a Prime Minister of State, or a great General of an Army" (*Prose Works,* III, 82 ff.). Thereupon, Swift writes his "Letter to Crassus," wherein we learn with considerable allegorical detail just how deeply Crassus-Marlborough is "stained with that odious and ignoble Vice of *Covetousness.*" In closing, Swift piously hopes that such a letter may serve to cure its recipient of "that little sordid Appetite, so utterly incon-sistent with all Pretences to a *Hero.*" This was by no means Swift's final comment on Marlborough or his downfall, but these two *Examiners* may be taken to exemplify his main lines of attack—first, the effort to show that Marlborough's services had been amply rewarded, and second, the attempt to demonstrate that the duke's personal faults justified his re-moval.

What is most striking in Swift's handling of the Marlborough affair is his boldness in attacking the duke as a man. As long as Marlborough had functioned as a victorious general, primarily outside the arena of domestic politics, he had enjoyed the hero's immunity to attack; but his increas-ingly political role, which eventually led to his dismissal, made him fair game, and Swift sensed that his audience was now ready to see the general cut down to size. It is true that Swift makes his initial approach gingerly, throwing off little more than indirect hints. Once the groundwork has been laid, however, he does not hesitate to point out the duke's personal blemishes, and to criticize his behavior. It is significant also that Swift emphasizes avarice as the duke's central failing. Excessive love of money is traditionally a vice of shopkeepers, rather than of gentlemen, and, as Swift insistently points out, it is a "little" vice, appropriate to little men. A charge of lechery, drunkenness, or irreligion would have been far less damaging to Marlborough's public image as a hero. On the whole, in his approach to the Marlborough controversy, as in so many of his political tracts, Swift is able to operate with the knowledge that once he points the way, his audience will willingly follow.

Unlike Swift, Defoe displays every sign of reluctance to discuss the subject of Marlborough's removal, though over the years the *Review* had frequently celebrated Marlborough's military triumphs, always with high praise for the general. His fall from grace posed for Defoe a particularly ticklish problem, for he was now obliged to offer, in one fashion or another, a defense of an action which to his Whig readers was indefensible. Much as he might have wanted to, the issue was not one Defoe could afford to ignore, and in the *Review* for January 22, 1712, he finally turns his attention to it. Defoe opens by remarking that he has received many "taunting Letters," sent by those who "would willingly lay a Snare" for him, asking for his thoughts on Marlborough's removal—a challenge he will now accept. In this opening we can see how Defoe pictures his readers' attitude toward him and toward the Marlborough dismissal. Although the *Review* was ostensibly neutral, Defoe had in the past served as a Tory apologist, assuring his readers that despite misleading labels, the Harley–St. John ministry was "Whig" in principle. Now he is on the defensive, sure that letters soliciting his views on the subject are meant to entrap him, for he is aware that his readers, already angry over what has happened to Marlborough, are ready to be equally angry at anyone who seeks to justify it.

By way of further preliminary, Defoe next goes on to remark:

. . . first to speak in general, I say this, if there is no Occasion for Displacing the Duke, I am sorry it is done, for the Nation's sake; and if there is an Occasion for it, I am doubly sorry for it, for his sake.

As to those who tremble at the Event of it, as if the Nation must fall . . . I have more hope in God's Goodness, and more Faith in the Protection promis'd to his Church, than to be of that Number; . . . [if a new leader is needed in the war] a proper General will be rais'd up by him that makes Men, and can make any Man a General. . . . [*Review,* VIII, 521 ff.]

These statements are designed with an eye toward the hostility Defoe anticipates. They are so general that no man could very well argue with them. At the same time, their net effect is to introduce a note of moderation in the discussion. Defoe regrets Marlborough's dismissal, yet by implication he admits that there may have been occasion for it. Likewise, his pious admonition that God can replace Marlborough if necessary serves as a gentle reminder to the *Review*'s Dissenter audience that Providence, which had played a considerable role in the duke's victories, might now be directing his defeat. On the other hand, Defoe goes on to add, he is emphatically opposed to those who "rejoyce" in Marlborough's plight, saying of them: "I abhorr the Principle, and can by no means join with the Men." Continuing in his carefully middle-of-the-road position, Defoe next praises Marlborough personally, though he balances his compliments with the reservation that he has never been "for making Man an Idol." The current attacks on the duke's character by those seeking to justify his removal, Defoe condemns as "Unjust and Dishonourable," for the removal "really needs no Justification at all." This latter statement, coming well along in the essay, is Defoe's first clear indication of his position, and he braces himself against his audience's annoyance by immediately following it with the remark: ". . . in this also I must explain myself, for I know what Age I speak in, and how readily Men put their own Interpretation upon other Men's Words."

No one will deny, says Defoe, that the queen possesses the authority to dismiss a general, so there need be no legal justification for the removal. As to the "Prudence of the Thing," Defoe goes on, "I am persuaded the greatest Guilt which has displac'd the Duke of *Marl———gh,* is the Error in Policy, and Prudence among his Friends." To illustrate his point, Defoe says he will cite two parallel examples from history. Actually, he gives three: (1) Mareschal de Biron was, in his early career, a faithful and devoted servant of Henry IV of France. So ardently did the French Protestants praise de Biron, however, that Henry was at last obliged in self-defense to destroy him as a dangerous rival. (2) Sir Thomas Cromwell helped Henry VIII introduce the reformation of religion in England. Henry did not want a complete reformation, however, and when those who wished a full break with Rome hailed Cromwell extravagantly as their champion, the king was forced to act, and Cromwell, "without any Fault in him," went down to ruin. (3) The story of the downfall of Essex in Queen Elizabeth's time is much the same, except that Essex began to believe his supporters' praises, and actually became guilty of revolt. The moral to be drawn from these examples is clear: ". . . nothing is so natural as to say, when People cry up any Man so high, as to tell their Sovereign she cannot act without them, it often works Mischief to the Person himself, by making it necessary to the Government to convince them of the Mistake." It is a tribute to the "Moderation and Temper which [Marlborough] is so much the Master of; and which adds the brightest part to his Glory . . . ," that he has not taken seriously "the Madness of the People" who praise him now.

What Defoe has done in this *Review* is, in effect, to beg the whole question. The crux of the Marlborough case, as the Whigs saw it, was an ethical one—was the queen *morally* justified in abruptly dismissing a man who had served her so well? Swift was quick to answer that she was; that the duke's services had been amply rewarded; and that his character was in fact such as to make him unfit to serve further. Defoe, on the other hand, has side-stepped this whole question and has instead manufactured a new issue—is it expedient for the duke's admirers to praise him so exuberantly? The reply Defoe gives is not one that would be likely to satisfy many indignant Marlborough supporters, nor, in all likelihood, did he expect it would. However, the answer does admirably serve to get Defoe out of a ticklish situation. It neither offends the *Review* audience irrevocably by criticizing the duke, nor compromises Defoe with the Harley ministry by criticizing the queen. Even the unspecified Marlborough enthusiasts whom Defoe condemns are pictured as sinning from a simple excess of zeal rather than from any evil designs, and Defoe's only unreserved criticism is directed at those who seek maliciously to calumniate the duke. Defoe's arguments reflect his delicate role as an apologist for a Tory ministry addressing a Whig audience—a role that necessitated a compromise between extremes which was far more real than Swift's professed moderation.

The difference between Swift's "moderation" and Defoe's may be further seen in the contrast between each man's use of a similar technique to demonstrate his middle-of-the-road position. Swift, in *Examiner* 28, and Defoe, in *Review* VIII, 203, resort to the same device—the printing of simultaneous abusive letters, one each from a violent Tory and a violent Whig. The reader is then invited to commiserate with the author whose moderate stance subjects him to fanatical attack from both sides. Swift introduces his letters by announcing that he thinks it proper to print copies of "two peculiar Letters, among many others" he has recently received in order to illustrate how he has been continually "worried on one Side by the *Whigs* for being too *severe;* and by the *Tories* on the other for being too *gentle*" (*Prose Works,* III, 88 ff.).

The first letter is from a Whig. It denounces *"Mr. Examiner"* as a *"Jesuit,"* employed by the friends of the Pretender to help introduce *"Popery* and *Slavery,* and *Arbitrary Power"* into England. The writer goes on to predict his own party's imminent return to power, and he concludes his letter by threatening Swift with assassination if he does not cease his attack on the deposed ministry. The letter from the Tory, who identifies himself as "a *Country Member,"* likewise expresses dissatisfaction with the *Examiner,* for, as he tells Swift, "It is plain you know a great deal more than you write; why will you not let us have it all out?" He goes on to urge Swift to expose more fully how the queen has been "treated with Insolence" by the Whigs, and how the Whig ministers "cheated" the nation "of several Millions." He ends his letter by remarking that although the Whig offenders deserve to be hanged, all that he demands is that they be revealed as the scoundrels they are.

The immediately noticeable thing about these two letters is the difference in intensity. The letter from the Whig is violent and abusive, while that of the Tory, despite its righteous indignation, is polite and restrained. In addition to his threat of murder, the Whig letterwriter manages to include three oaths (two "D-mme"s and one "by G-d") in his brief note. The Tory, on the other hand, is not only subdued in language, but even goes so far as to disavow violent intentions. The weighting of the scales is doubly apparent when we consider the strong probability that Swift himself composed the letter ostensibly sent him by the Whig. Certain phrases in the letter seem rather too carefully designed for ironic emphasis of the letterwriter's fanaticism and his ignoble motives. For example, at one point he warns Swift that he and his friends "will take the first proper Occasion to *cut your Throat,* as all such Enemies to *Moderation* ought to be served" and later he complains, "It is enough to lose our Power and Employments, without setting the whole Nation against us." Likewise, the letter furnishes a suspiciously convenient example of certain of the stylistic sins Swift had criticized earlier in his comments on style in the *Tatler.*[9] Specifically, the Whig letterwriter uses the word *"Bamboozzle,"* which Swift had singled out as offensive, and, in a letter of only 230 words, he manages to crowd in the following cliches: *"as clear as the Sun at Noon-Day," "every Dog hath his Day,"* and *"sleep in a whole Skin,"* each of which he has obligingly italicized for us.

There is no doubt that Swift received many abusive letters from Whig partisans, but nevertheless, the one he chooses to quote seems a little too appropriate to be altogether true. Whether Swift also may have composed the Tory letter is less clear, but one thing at any rate is apparent—had Swift really been interested in exhibiting Tory extremism, specimens far better than the one he offers were available. A genuine or manufactured letter from a Jacobite or a High-Flier, for example, would have served admirably to balance the hysteria of the Whig letter. Commenting on the letters he has printed, Swift speaks of himself as "taking the Medium between these Extreams," but it is obvious that he intends his readers to see the Whig letterwriter as a crazed fanatic, and the Tory correspondent as nothing more than a justifiably excited gentleman.

On July 10, 1712, about seventeen months after Swift had printed his opposing letters, Defoe turned to the same device in the *Review*. Swift's example may even have suggested the idea to Defoe, though as a means for demonstrating one's moderation, the technique is as old as rhetoric. "It was but two Days ago," says Defoe,

. . . that I receiv'd at one and the same time, one Letter from a Passionate Whig, and another from a Furious *Jacobite;* the one Threatning me with the Gallows, when *their Party* gets up again; and the other with Murther and Assassination immediately, after the manner of *John Tutchin.* [*Review*, VIII, 813 ff.]

After asking the reader, "What can more testifie to me that I am in the Right, than that the Mad-Men on both Sides are thus Enrag'd?" Defoe goes on to print the Jacobite's letter. As is appropriate for a supporter of the exiled Pretender, the author writes in French. His letter, which Defoe tells us requires no translation, is sufficiently brief to bear quotation in full.

Revieu, June 14. 1712.
De Foe,
   Quelle Fuire Infernalle, & quel Demon t'ont Inspirré le Poizon du Mensonge, que tu Vomit aujourdhuy, contre la Pierre que les ouvriers ont Rejettée[;] souvien toy Esprit Malin, que cette pierre, sera un jour la clef du Cintre? La Sedition que tu publie tous les jours te Causera un Chastiment, quel te souvien de ton Predesseseur Tutchin, come il fut Bastoné per ses Infames Libelles, Engense de Viperre, quant cesseras tu, d'insulter les Tests

Couronnée, dont ta est Enemy mortel; ausy bien que ceux dont tu espouse le
Party? Tu est un Miserable chien quy ne fait que hurler.

Nigro

Against these charges, Defoe defends himself briefly, maintaining that
though he is unalterably opposed to the Pretender politically, he has
always been open and honest in his enmity and has never resorted to any
personal abuse.

Defoe next turns to "the other Scurrilous Gentleman," but instead of
giving the second letter in full, he merely comments upon two of the
points it raises. His Whig letterwriter, Defoe tells us, first warns that a
reckoning with the Harley ministry is soon due, and that if Defoe
continues to defend Tory policies, he will find that *"Tyburn will be worse
than the Pillory."* Defoe vigorously denies the imputed Tory bias, and
professes surprise that a man like himself, "who dares stand in the Pillory
rather than betray his Friends, *the Whigs,* must expect *Tyburn* from them
in Reward; whenever he presumes to tell them freely their own Mistakes." We next learn that the Whig letterwriter, having written that " 'a
War with *Holland* would be, as if one Arm should Wound another,' "
goes on to accuse Defoe of urging such a war. In his defense, Defoe
quotes an earlier *Review* in which he had himself remarked, " 'That a
War with *Holland* at this Time, I should esteem no otherwise, than of a
Man cutting off his Left Arm with his Right. . . .' " Thus, Defoe points
out with understandable indignation, his Whig correspondent has not
only made a demonstrably false charge, but has added injury to insult by
phrasing it in an image borrowed from the very man he accuses. Defoe
then reiterates his opposition to war with the Dutch, and denies that he
writes as a Tory propagandist, disingenuously remarking that

. . . throughout the whole course of this Ministry, I have neither written, or
forborn to write one VVord by the Direction of the Ministry, or to oblige or
serve any Party; nor have I directly or indirectly been paid or rewarded for so
doing; . . . the Circumstances I labour under in the VVorld, might, one
would think, deliver me from the Suspicion of this Slander.

He closes with the promise that despite the threats of "hot implacable
Whigs [and] of Exasperated Inveterate *Jacobites,*" he will continue to tell
the truth as he sees it.

It is noteworthy that Defoe's Whig and Tory correspondents come far closer to representing the real political extremes than do those of Swift. Both correspondents threaten Defoe with violence, and each is clearly an irrational fanatic, though it is true that the Whig letter, insofar as it is conveyed to us, is less abusive in tone and language than its Tory counterpart. As in the case of Swift, it is overwhelmingly probable that Defoe composed the letters himself. It seems rather too pat, for example, that the advocate of the Pretender should so clearly emphasize his treasonous affiliation by writing his letter in French, especially since the French in question is not the educated, aristocratic French one might expect from a Jacobite, but rather an anglicized, pidgin French that any but the humblest of Defoe's readers could readily decipher.

In any case, it is clear that Defoe, like Swift, has taken care to print only such charges against himself as are easily answerable or require no defense. To be attacked as an enemy of the Pretender, Defoe knew, could only enhance him in the eyes of his audience. Accordingly, he proudly admits his "guilt," denying only that he has indulged in personal libel. The charges made by the Whig, on the other hand, if believed, could have been extremely damaging; but Defoe has seen to it that the first of these charges (that he advocated a war with Holland) is so easily refuted that greater weight is added to his denial of the second (that he was a hireling of the Tories). It is significant also that while Swift's letters are addressed merely to an unidentified *"Mr. Examiner,"* Defoe's Jacobite addresses him by name, and the Whig correspondent makes specific reference to Defoe's experience in the pillory after the publication of the *Shortest Way With Dissenters.* Defoe's public reputation as a Dissenter who had suffered imprisonment for an anti-High-Flier tract was one of his strongest recommendations with his tradesman audience, and he does not hesitate to use it, along with his self-advertised poverty, in support of his claims that he is unsubsidized by the Tory ministers.

That Defoe was, in fact, literally in the pay of Harley, makes his position doubly ironic, for as I have tried to show, in comparing the two men as pamphleteers, the nature of Defoe's audience required that he play a more truly "moderate" role than Swift, who accepted no money, but whose audience, in turn, necessitated a brand of Toryism considerably more zealous than Defoe's. These two audiences—country squiredom and the commercial middle class—comprised two crucial centers of political power in Queen Anne's day, and the survival of the Harley ministry depended equally upon Swift's ability in arousing the first and Defoe's success in placating the second. Happily, each man's personal convictions coincided with the requirements of his task. Both performed their jobs with consummate skill, and when, despite their efforts, a combination of internal dissension and the queen's unexpected death resulted in the Tory downfall, each could look back in legitimate satisfaction at his own considerable share in paving the way to the Peace of Utrecht.

Seven: "That the Truth of Things May Be
Transmitted to Future Ages":
History and Crisis in the Tory Tracts

T HE bulk of this study has been devoted to examining the
techniques and approaches Swift employed in conveying to the readers of
his political tracts something of his own heightened sense of urgency over
the nation's future. As we have seen, Swift's Tory tracts, to a greater
extent than any of his previous writings, were composed with specific
audiences and persuasive goals in mind. In the course of my discussion I
have indicated how often it is necessary to discount Swift's insistent
pretense that he writes primarily as a historian with an eye to future
generations. Whatever Swift may have declared, his contemporaries were
well aware that they, and not posterity, were his most immediate targets.
"The title of an history is too pompous for such a performance," Lord
Orrery remarks concerning the *Four Last Years of the Queen,*" but as a
pamphlet, it will appear the best defence of Lord OXFORD's administration, and the clearest account of the treaty of *Utrecht,* that has hitherto
been written." [1]

Even Swift would later admit by implication that his Tory tracts were
ephemeral. There exists a letter of November 22, 1737, to Swift from
Charles Ford, in which Ford, evidently responding to a comment of
Swift's, writes:

I hear they are going to publish two volumes more of your works. I see no
reason why all the pamphlets published at the end of the Queen's reign might
not be inserted. Your objection of their being momentary things will not
hold. *Killing no Murder* [an anti-Cromwellian tract by Edward
Sexby—1657], and many other old tracts, are still read with pleasure. . . . [2]

Yet it would be a mistake to discount totally Swift's frequent public
avowals that he wrote primarily for an audience unborn. The claim is

114

disingenuous, but nevertheless, it expresses an underlying intent that was to become increasingly serious as Swift's tract-writing career progressed. Swift had always been interested in history, and even while still in the employ of Sir William Temple he had composed extensive abstracts (some of which still exist) of English history. These abstracts consist largely of notes made from Samuel Daniel's *Collection of the History of England* and from Temple's *Introduction to the History of England,* of which Swift at one time planned a continuation.[3] When the post of historiographer royal fell vacant early in 1714, Swift, who had already written the majority of his Tory tracts, immediately applied for the position. His motive, Swift explained in his petition to the queen, was not the salary (which was small) but a desire to leave an honest record of her reign for posterity—a task he had presumably already partially accomplished in works like the *Conduct of the Allies* and in the manuscript he was later to call the *History of the Four Last Years of the Queen.* As his formal request points out:

The change of ministry about four years ago, the fall of the Duke of Marlborough, and the proceedings since, . . . are all capable of being very maliciously represented to posterity, if they should fall under the pen of some writer of the opposite party, as they probably may.

Upon these reasons, it is necessary, for the honour of the Queen and in justice to her servants, that some able hand should be immediately employed to write the history of her Majesty's reign; that the truth of things may be transmitted to future ages, and bear down the falsehood of malicious pens. [*Prose Works,* VIII, 200]

Swift's conviction that, unless steps were taken, the story of Anne's reign would "probably" be written by some triumphant Whig author, reflects his gloomy anticipation of the disaster that was clearly in store for the moribund ministry. The quarrel between Harley and St. John, despite Swift's desperate attempts to heal it, had by this time progressed to open warfare. The ailing queen was in visible decline (she was to die within weeks of Swift's petition), and John Partridge himself could have safely predicted that the Tory ministry was doomed. In these circumstances, Swift could only expect that the flood of barbarism he had sought to stem was about to inundate the country. He could and would continue to write tracts designed to reverse that flood, but a strong subsidiary purpose had developed in his mind. He became obsessed with the truism that the victors always write the histories, and it now became a major ambition of his to make sure, while there was still time, that posterity received at least one full and true account of the ministry's good fight. As David Nichol Smith has said:

His pamphlets and all his writings as a politician—if we interpret the evidence aright—was of small importance in his eyes compared with the record which he hoped to leave to posterity of the greatness of the reign of Anne. As he foresaw his career while his party was still in power, this History was to be his greatest work.[4]

At the outset of his career, in his address to "Prince Posterity" in the *Tale of a Tub,* Swift had his fatuous "author" remark that he had originally hoped to accumulate a list of writers and works that were certain to last forever; unfortunately, he had put the task off for a day, and the names had slipped from his mind. Enquiry among readers and booksellers proved in vain, for the *"Memorial of them was lost among Men, their Place was no more to be found"* (*Prose Works,* I, 21). Posterity, presumably, could bear such a loss with composure, but behind the joke lies Swift's early awareness of a genuine problem—if historical truth is not somehow recorded, for all practical purposes it ceases to exist; or alternately, it may be recorded, but in so warped a fashion as to be worthless. After viewing the spirits of the dead in Glubbdubdrib, Gulliver finds himself

. . . chiefly disgusted with modern History. For having strictly examined all the Persons of greatest Name in the Courts of Princes for an Hundred Years past, I found how the World had been misled by prostitute Writers. . . .

Here I discovered the Roguery and Ignorance of those who pretend to write *Anecdotes,* or secret History; who send so many Kings to their Graves with a Cup of Poison; will repeat the Discourse between a Prince and chief Minister, where no Witness was by. . . . Here I discovered the true Causes of many great Events that have surprized the World: How a Whore can govern the Back-stairs, the Back-stairs a Council, and the Council a Senate. [*Prose Works,* XI, 199]

After such an experience, it is not surprising that a few pages later Gulliver, when asked how he would behave if he had the immortality of a Struldbrugg, announces:

. . . I would carefully record every Action and Event of Consequence that happened in the Publick, impartially draw the Characters of the several

Successions of Princes, and great Ministers of State; with my own Observations on every Point. I would exactly set down the several Changes in Customs, Language, Fashion of Dress, Dyet and Diversions. By all which Acquirements, I should be a living Treasury of Knowledge and Wisdom. . . . [*Prose Works,* XI, 209]

It is in keeping with this attitude that one of Swift's declared motives in proposing an English Academy was the fear that if language were allowed to continue to change as it had in the past, in about two hundred years the histories describing the "Glory of Her Majesty's Reign" (*Prose Works,* IV, 17) might become largely unintelligible.

Swift was to be disappointed both in his hopes for the post of historiographer royal and in his ambitions to write a definitive account of Anne's reign. The closest he was to come to the full-scale history he had hoped would be his monument was in his admittedly imperfect Tory tracts and in the few retrospective memoirs he composed during and immediately after the collapse of the Harley–St. John ministry in 1714. Though in all these works Swift's role as a historian is peripheral to his more central functions as a polemicist and apologist, it is nevertheless possible to derive—especially from the larger works, such as the *Four Last Years of the Queen*—some idea of the light in which Swift viewed the task of ensuring "that the truth of things . . . be transmitted to future ages."

If by "history" we mean primarily an accurate register of facts and events, free of overt bias and supported by close research, then Swift's Tory writings will obviously not qualify. Though valuable in themselves as historical documents and as sources of information, the record they offer is too imbalanced and their author too much the emotionally committed partisan for us to accept him as the disinterested chronicler this definition implies. To Lord Orrery's statement concerning the *Four Last Years of the Queen* (quoted earlier) we may add the comment of Lord Chesterfield, who, in a letter of May 11, 1758, to George Faulkner, said of the same work:

As for the History, . . . to tell you the truth, it is only a compilation of party pamphlets. I have good authority for what I now say, for Lord Bolingbroke, who had seen the original manuscript, told me that it consisted chiefly of the lies of the day, which they had in seeming confidence communicated to the Dean to write *Examiners* and party pamphlets upon, and which the Dean took as authentic materials for history.[5]

Though it is hard to believe that St. John would have put the case in terms as grossly unfair to Swift as those that Chesterfield reports, it is true enough that for much of his information Swift was dependent upon the facts that the ministers chose to give him, and inevitably those facts were the ones which the ministers most desired to see publicized. Swift was neither a simple hireling who could be ordered to write whatever expediency demanded nor a naïve tool who would credulously pass on any and all dubious matters the ministers conveyed to him. But aside from the distortions which his own bias introduced, the Tory tracts do show evidence of how Harley and St. John—particularly the latter—were able on occasion to manipulate Swift's interpretations by a combination of suggestion and selective information.[6]

As formal history, then, Swift's Tory writings will not rate very highly; but if we conceive of the historian's task as extending beyond the accurate presentation of data, Swift's claim to the title of "historian" becomes more than a mere rhetorical convenience. For the sort of history which Swift hoped to leave for posterity was less a straightforward record of fact than an instructive dramatic narration of a climactic moment in the national life. If, as Swift believed, the course of history was generally cyclical, it followed that certain recurrent patterns of crisis, provoked by the unchanging wellsprings of human ambition and appetite, would reappear with some regularity. In such a view, the ancient belief that history is valuable not merely as a means of recovering the past but as a way of illuminating the present assumes a central importance, and it becomes a crucial function of the writer of history (especially of contemporary history) to perceive and to explicate the precise ways in which history continually repeats itself.

We have seen how in his Tory tracts Swift, like most of his fellow pamphleteers, repeatedly turns to historical analogy as a means of interpreting current situations and policies. Obviously the value of such interpretation depends upon the validity of the parallel, and the reader, if he is to be properly instructed, must be on constant guard to detect the plausible but false analogies which biased or misinformed historians will put forward. If the historian is to analyze contemporary events correctly for his readers, he will need more than a thorough knowledge of the past and a mind unclouded (at least initially) by partisanship; he will need a detailed and preferably first-hand knowledge of affairs and of the complex ways in which the course of momentous public occurrences can sometimes be determined by such seemingly trivial influences as a general's greed, a prime minister's sense of social inferiority, or a governor's taste in mistresses. Swift, as Ehrenpreis has put it,

. . . inclined toward a deep split between appearance and actuality in his analysis of historical incidents. He felt obsessed by a doctrine which Bacon states in milder terms than he: that God 'doth hang the greatest weight upon the smallest wires, *maxima e minimis suspendens.*' Swift loved to dwell on the mighty consequences of tiny events.[7]

It is not surprising to learn that Swift's taste in historical reading ran toward memoirs, eye-witness accounts of secret transactions, and revelations of the "now it can be told" variety. It will be recalled that Swift, when he professes to write as nothing more than an aroused patriot (as in the *Conduct of the Allies*), stresses the public nature of his facts; but when he assumes the title of "historian" (as in the *Four Last Years of the Queen*), he writes as an insider, a participant with special private knowledge of events and the men who shaped them. Only to such a historian would the full truth be accessible, and only on the basis of such truth could valid historical analogies be derived.

The particular glory of Anne's reign which Swift was so anxious to record before the truth was drowned in a flood of Whig falsifications was the triumphant manner in which the queen and her loyal ministers had thwarted (if only temporarily) the treasonous plans of ruthlessly ambitious men who, like their historical analogues from Satan onward, were willing to plunge society into ruinous disorder in an attempt to satisfy their lust for power. Sir William Temple, from whom Swift learned much of history, had described in his essay *Of Popular Discontents* the classic pattern in which these seditious movements proceed. There will always be occasions, whether real or imaginary (Temple writes), for popular unrest and grievance against the monarch. Such occasions will create opportunities for those

. . . who cover their own ends under those of the public, and, by the good and service of the nation, mean nothing but their own. The practice begins of knaves upon fools, of artificial and crafty men upon the simple and the good; these easily follow, and are caught, while the others lay trains, and pursue a game, wherein they design no other share, than of toil and danger to their company, but the gain and the quarry wholly to themselves.

They blow up sparks that fall in by chance, or could not be avoided, or else throw them in wherever they find the stubble is dry: they find out miscarriages wherever they are, and forge them often where they are not; they quarrel first with the officers, and then with the prince or the state; sometimes with the execution of laws, and at others with the institutions, how ancient and sacred soever. They make fears pass for dangers, and appearances for truth; represent misfortunes for faults, and mole-hills for mountains; and by the persuasions of the vulgar, and pretences of patriots, or lovers of their country, at the same time they undermine the credit and authority of the government, and set up their own. This raises a faction between those subjects that would support it, and those that would ruin it; or rather between those that possess the honours and advantages of it, and those that, under the pretence of reforming, design only or chiefly to change the hands it is in, and care little what becomes of the rest.[8]

To preserve stability and social continuity against such disruptive movements was, as Swift saw it, one of government's most important tasks. Given man's instinctive corrupt nature and the downward drift it fostered, social change of almost any sort (unless it involved a careful return to an earlier standard) was apt to be for the worse. Since civilization and its values were extremely fragile, it was only through a constant vigilance and control that society could hope to hold its own and prevent disorder and its attendant dangers. This attitude lies behind statements like that made by St. John in a letter to Swift on September 12, 1724. In reply to Swift's bantering accusation of atheism, St. John remarks that he looks upon freethinkers as "the Pests of Society, because their endeavours are directed to losen the bands of it, & to take att least one curb [i.e., religion] out of the mouth of that wild Beast Man when it would be well if he was check'd by half a score others" (*Correspondence,* III, 27).

What lies in wait for society when the natural corruption of "that wild Beast Man" is allowed free rein is most graphically illustrated by Swift in his portrait of the Yahoos. The Yahoos, as Gulliver is at last reluctantly forced to admit, are humans, possibly even the descendants of a shipwrecked European crew. Gulliver goes so far as to conjecture from their facial characteristics that originally they may perhaps have been Englishmen. The lesson is obvious, even to Gulliver—Yahoodom, from which some men have painfully raised themselves, is never more than one step away, waiting to re-embrace them, and once man is freed from the restraints of society and religion, his predictable descent into a nightmare world of chaos and bestial anarchy is frighteningly quick. As Swift was to point out in the *Modest Proposal,* only the finest of distinctions makes the English policy of gobbling up the wealth of the Irish superior to a cannibalism of a more literal sort.

To the adherents of such a view of human nature, it seemed axiomatic that the nation's well-being was largely dependent upon the degree to which the proper social order was maintained. Somewhere between the monarch at the top of the social pyramid and the great mass of the population at its broad base, the middle class, the gentry, and the aristocracy (along with all their infinitely complex subdivisions) occupied their respective proper levels, each with its natural function and sphere of operation. As Swift remarks in his sermon *On Mutual Subjection:*

The Prince cannot say to the Merchant, I have no need of thee; nor the Merchant to the Labourer, I have no need of thee. . . . [God] hath assigned every Man his particular Station to be useful in Life; and this for the Reason given by the Apostle, *that there may be no Schism in the Body.* [*Prose Works,* IX, 143]

In such a scheme, no man or class could rise except at the expense of another, and to do so was not only to disrupt society, but to violate a divinely sanctioned order. For hierarchy, as Swift's sermon indicates, was considered a basic principle of the universe. The human social order had its counterparts among both the angels above man and the animals below him. Thus, in 1710 when Swift chides the would-be wits who had "answered" the *Tale of a Tub,* he finds a natural analogy close at hand in "The dull, unwieldy, ill-shaped Ox [who] would needs put on the Furniture of a Horse, not considering he was born to Labour, to plow the Ground for the Sake of superior Beings, and that he has neither the Shape, Mettle nor Speed of that nobler Animal he would affect to personate" (*Prose Works,* I, 8). The same idea, this time expressed in human terms, occurs sixteen years later in *Gulliver's Travels* when Gulliver, seeing that his boasting elicits only laughter from the Brobdingnagians, is led to reflect upon

. . . how vain an Attempt it is for a Man to endeavour doing himself Honour among those who are out of all Degree of Equality or Comparison with him. And yet I have seen the Moral of my own Behaviour very frequent in

England since my Return; where a little contemptible Varlet, without the least Title to Birth, Person, Wit, or common Sense, shall presume to look with Importance, and put himself upon a Foot with the greatest Persons of the Kingdom.[9]

Swift's animus against the "Stock-Jobbers" and the "Monied-Interest" in his Tory tracts reflects his sharply increased sense of alarm after 1710 over what he saw as perhaps the major single threat to England's hierarchical stability—the extent to which a growing and vigorous middle class had been encroaching upon such traditional centers of power as the landed gentry, the hereditary aristocracy, and even the crown itself. In *Intelligencer* 9 (1728) Swift was to ask, "how it comes about, that for above sixty Years past, the chief Conduct of Affairs in [England] hath been generally placed in the Hands of *New-men,* with few Exceptions?" He goes on to answer by explaining that during the Civil Wars many great families suffered near extinction, so that middle-class inroads into formerly exclusive preserves of power became difficult to avoid. "I date from this Aera . . . the Necessity the Crown lay under of introducing *New-men* into the highest Employments of State, or to the Office of what we now call Prime Ministers . . . merely for Want of a Supply among the Nobility" (*Prose Works,* XII, 47).

Among the *"New-men"* who had acceded to office was Lord Somers, and in measuring the growth of Swift's concern over the threat to the hierarchical principle, it is informative to trace his changing attitude toward Somers' respectable but nonaristocratic origins. In the dedication of the *Tale of a Tub,* Swift does not discreetly ignore Somers' prosaic background, as most panegyrists of the time would have done; rather, he makes it the occasion for a somewhat equivocal compliment delivered in the form of a mock-complaint in which the dedicator expresses his chagrin at having failed to discover any *new* qualities for which to praise the universally admired Somers. He explains that he had hoped in his dedication to surprise the world by some such device as tracing Somers' "Pedigree . . . in a Lineal Descent from the House of *Austria"* (*Prose Works,* I, 15), but instead he has been obliged to resort to the "old beaten Story" of Somers' many other brilliant qualities. The implication behind the raillery here is that Swift, unlike the obtuse bookseller who is the ostensible author of the dedication, is more impressed by personal virtue than by lofty ancestry. Yet, it is significant that Swift chose to mention the topic at all, especially in circumstances where only the most unreserved praise was expected. If Swift's later interpretation of Somers' character is correct, the Whig lord must have found Swift's reference to his lineage tactless even in a compliment.

By the time Swift came to write the *Four Last Years of the Queen* he had served three years as a Tory pamphleteer, and pedigree had become one of his major concerns. In the Characters of the Whig leaders which open that work, Swift emphasizes such things as the plebian background of a Godolphin ("originally intended for a Trade") and the leveling principles of a Sunderland (who "hoped to see the Day, when there should not be a Peer in *England*"). But it is Somers in particular who receives this treatment, for his lowly origins, as Swift sees it, are the key to his entire conduct. Swift explains that Somers owes his career to "Republican" politicians who, recognizing that "the Nobility and Gentry would probably adhere to the Established Church, and to the Rights of Monarchy as delivered down from their Ancestors," made it a practice to introduce men like Somers, who "were perfectly indifferent to any or no Religion; and, who were not likely to inherit much Loyalty from those to whom they owed their Birth" (*Prose Works,* VII, 5). Swift finds that Somers' dominant characteristic, formality, is only natural in a man who is justifiably sensitive over his "humble Original" and who accordingly "keeps all Familiarity at the utmost distance." Six years later, in a letter of December 19, 1719, to St. John, Swift repeats this explanation, referring to Somers as one whose "consciousness of a mean extraction" (*Correspondence,* II, 333) served to keep him regular in morals and manners. Swift's final comment on Somers' ancestry occurs in a marginal note jotted in a copy of John Macky's *Characters of the Court of Britain* (1733): Macky had written that Somers came from a "CREDITABLE FAMILY," to which Swift appends the curt explication: ". . . very mean, his father was a noted Rogue" (*Prose Works,* V, 258).

In fact, this man whose origins Swift so despised came from a respectable middle-class background not unlike Swift's own. However, as a representative of the self-made men who had elbowed their way into positions of power normally occupied by more genealogically prepossessing figures, Somers symbolized for Swift a terrible threat to the traditional social order. Swift was not so slavish an admirer of the nobility that he considered it the exclusive repository of virtue. Yet, he did feel that

. . . if there be any Difference between human Creatures in the Point of *natural parts* . . . it should seem, that the Advantage lies on the Side of Children born from noble and wealthy Parents; the same traditional Sloth and Luxury, which renders their Bodies weak and effeminate, perhaps refining and giving a freer Motion to the Spirits, beyond what can be expected from the gross, robust Issue of meaner Mortals. [*Prose Works,* XII, 48]

That the aristocracy and gentry might benefit from a periodic infusion of new blood from socially inferior, but physically sturdier, classes was an idea Swift recognized as practical and even necessary. As Gulliver explains to his Houyhnhnm master, noble families in England nearly always die out after three generations, "unless the Wife take Care to provide a healthy Father among her Neighbours, or Domesticks, in order to improve and continue the Breed." * But an occasional therapeutic infusion of new blood was one thing; wholesale infiltration with eventual complete displacement of the aristocracy and gentry was quite another, and the latter, in Swift's view, was a real danger posed by the leveling spirit and practice of men like Somers.

At the head of society was the king, who had in earlier days wielded a power which, in theory, if not in practice, was both absolute and sacred. The hereditary right of one family to rule the nation had in the recent past been justified by the theory of Divine Right. By Swift's day, however, the steps taken to ensure the Protestant succession made such an explanation at least partially untenable. Accordingly, when Swift defends the hereditary nature of the throne, as he does in the *Sentiments of a Church-of-England Man,* he appeals to expediency rather than religion, pointing out that the crown must remain inheritable, "not from any intrinsick Merit, or unalienable Right in a *particular Family;* but [in order] to avoid the Consequences that usually attend the Ambition of

* *Prose Works,* XI, 256. Gulliver's statement is based on ample evidence, since on his earlier voyage to Glubbdubdrib he had examined the ancestral spirits of several noble families and had been much surprised to find a predominance of "Pages, Lacqueys, Valets, Coachmen, Gamesters, Fidlers, Players, Captains, and Pick-pockets" (*Prose Works,* XI, 199). As this passage and Gulliver's later remark to his Houyhnhnm master show, Swift was not without his cynicism toward claims of exalted lineage. But to see only the deflationary intent of these passages is to miss the basic point, for Swift expected his readers, like himself, to be more appalled than amused by the degree to which aristocratic purity had already been compromised.

Competitors . . . (*Prose Works,* II, 18). But although in Swift's time English monarchs and their apologists had learned to be discreet about mentioning the Divine Right to rule, for many in the early eighteenth century the king still retained a considerable aura of semidivinity. Among the ancient "proofs" of the divine sanction attending monarchs had been their reputed power to cure victims of "the King's Evil" (scrofula) by an application of the royal hands. Anne was the last English ruler to perform this ritual, and it is significant that Swift had enough faith in its efficacy to solicit the influence of the Duchess of Ormonde in hopes of getting a friend's son "touched for the evil" by the queen.[10]

By 1702, when Anne assumed the throne, the royal prerogative had been much eroded and, against the bitter opposition of many Tories, was in the process of being eroded further still. Despite his veneration of the monarchy, Swift was himself dubious about the High-Flier doctrine which held that since the monarch could, by definition, do no public wrong, passive obedience to royal whim was obligatory in all circumstances. Swift's theory of government, as described in *Contests and Dissensions, Sentiments of a Church-of-England Man,* and elsewhere, is one in which ruling power is divided between the king (representing the broad interests of the nation), the House of Lords (representing the hereditary aristocracy), and the House of Commons (representing the land- and property-owning classes). Ideally the powers of these three branches of government should be in perfect balance. Each of the three, jealous of its own power, will act as a check against the encroachments of the others, and in this way, the impulse to tyranny, always potential in all wielders of power, will be guarded against. Yet, Swift insisted that even in such an arrangement it was essential that the king should retain possession of the final edge of decisive power—a power to be used at royal discretion when circumstances required.

In any system where "order" is the greatest social virtue, it becomes vitally necessary that there be an ultimate authority beyond which there can be no appeal. Admittedly, monarchs might often be anything but wise; yet Swift believed that the principle of authority embodied in even an incompetent or evil king was more important than any individual. Thus, the king, in what was perhaps his most important single function, served as the nation's final arbiter, and in so doing provided the moral center of gravity which kept society stable. The exercise of authority was not merely the king's prerogative; it was his duty. Royal indecisiveness or reluctance to assert the powers of the throne could create a vacuum which, as Temple had pointed out, ambitious men would seek to fill, and the ensuing disruptions in the hierarchy would be the first steps in a degenerative process which, if unchecked, could endanger the entire fabric of society.

These ideas concerning social stability and its enemies were basic to most Augustan conservative political thought. They have been recently explicated by Bernard S. Schilling in his *Dryden and the Conservative Myth,* which offers a close reading of Dryden's *Absalom and Achitophel* as a dramatic restatement of the principles of order and authority.[11] It is interesting in this connection to note how Swift, as he presents the basic political drama of Queen Anne's reign, follows a general pattern similar to that of Dryden's poem. Though elements matching those of the Dryden poem may be found in the majority of Swift's Tory pamphlets, the parallel becomes clearest when Swift is most consciously functioning as a historian—namely, in the *History of the Four Last Years of the Queen.* King David, as Dryden portrays him at the opening of *Absalom and Achitophel,* is possessed of almost every desirable royal quality except one—decisiveness. He is a benevolent king, lenient and normally disinclined toward exercising his full authority. But David's lack of self-assertiveness, although a private virtue, comes close to being a public disaster, for it is the king's function to wield power, and failure to do so gives occasion and hope to those who wish to usurp royal authority. The rebellious Achitophel himself recognizes this fact, and he tells Absalom:

> Not that your Father's Mildness I contemn;
> But manly Force becomes the Diadem.
> 'Tis true, he grants the People all they crave;
> And more perhaps than Subjects ought to have:
> For Lavish grants suppose a Monarch tame,
> And more his Goodness than his Wit proclaim.
> But when shoud People strive their Bonds to break,
> If not when Kings are Negligent or Weak?
>   (381–88)[12]

The character of Queen Anne, as it emerges in the *Four Last Years,* is much like David's. She too is a paragon in everything except her reluctance to use her royal power. Even before his Tory career Swift had detected and, by implication, had mildly admonished this quality in the queen. In the *Project for the Advancement of Religion* Swift, after copious praise of the queen, goes on to remark: "How would it brighten Her Character to the present and after Ages, if she would exert Her utmost Authority to instil [*sic*] some Share of those Virtues into Her People, which they are too degenerate to learn only from Her Example" (*Prose Works,* II, 62). In the same way, throughout his 1710–14 tracts written for public consumption Swift is obliged to be circumspect, and so he merely suggests that Anne's indecisiveness, like David's, is due to an excess of modesty and amiability. In the *Journal to Stella,* however, and in the later retrospective tracts not written for immediate publication, Swift makes it clear that his private opinion of the queen's irresolution was less charitable. In *Some Free Thoughts,* for example, he speaks of "the uncertain timorous Nature of the Queen," and in *An Enquiry into the Behaviour of the Queen's Last Ministry* he argues that Anne's "dubious Management" and fondness for "moderating Schemes" were the original causes of the Tory downfall (*Prose Works,* VIII, 82, 152, 160).

In Dryden's poem, the major beneficiary of David's good-natured leniency is Absalom, whose faults the king "coud not, or . . . woud not see" (36). The analogous situation in Swift is that between the queen and her erstwhile favorite, the Duke of Marlborough, though Swift's attitude, in the circumstances, is far less indulgent than Dryden's toward Absalom. Marlborough and Absalom are both military heroes (of Absalom, we are told: "Early in Foreign fields he won Renown, / With Kings and States ally'd to *Israel*'s Crown"—23–24), and each is much favored by his kindly monarch. The results in both cases are the same— ingratitude and, eventually, treasonous designs upon the throne. The suggestion that Marlborough wished to usurp the crown originated with Swift, and it will be recalled that the inclusion of this startling charge in the *Four Last Years* was one of the factors which led to the delay in that work's publication.

There is no individual parallel in Swift's tracts for Achitophel, though it could be argued that the members of the Whig Junto play this role collectively. These, resolved like Achitophel "to Ruine or to Rule the State" (174), choose as their major weapon a protracted and costly war. Achitophel's scheme for dethroning David is precisely the sort Swift ascribes to the Whig lords and their "Stock-Jobber" friends: Achitophel says he will plunge David

> deep in some Expensive War;
> Which when his Treasure can no more Supply,
> He must, with the Remains of Kingship, buy.
>
> (394–96)

In Swift, as in Dryden, the "rebellion" is pictured as attracting a group of malcontents, with a range that includes almost every major form of religious and social extremism. In either case the one attitude which unites the motley insurgents is their dissatisfaction with the distribution of power in a society that recognizes the monarch's authority as ultimate this side of heaven. In seeking to alter the established patterns of society, Swift's "embittered Faction" either forgets or chooses to ignore the fact that "all great Changes have the same Effect upon Commonwealths that Thunder hath upon Liquors; making the *Dregs* fly up to the Top" (*Prose Works,* III, 65). From the same philosophical basis Dryden cautions the Jebusites that "All other Errors but disturb a State; / But Innovation is the Blow of Fate" (799–800).

Queen Anne is not without her friends and wise counselors, the equivalents of men like Dryden's Zadoc. Harley and St. John apprise the queen of the dangers in the situation, just as Zadoc and his friends are described as warning David:

> as their Duty bound,
> They shew'd the King the danger of the Wound;
> That no Concessions from the Throne woud please,
> But Lenitives fomented the Disease.
>
> (923–26)

The dramatic climax of the *Four Last Years* comes near the end, when the queen finally orders the Duke of Ormonde to engage in no further battles while peace negotiations continue.[13] Before this point, the queen's patience and leniency have been stressed, but with this action she becomes firm and dominant. In terms of Dryden's poem, this situation is analogous to David's final thundering speech, wherein he reasserts his royal authority. " 'Tis time I shew I am not good by Force" (950), says David, and, "by Heav'n inspir'd" (936), he declares his intentions to crush the rebellion; "For Lawfull Pow'r is still Superiour found, / When long driven back, at length it stands the ground" (1024–25). Since *Absalom and Achitophel* and the *Four Last Years* were both written during the course of the power struggles they describe, neither Dryden nor Swift could offer his readers a final resolution of the conflict. Dryden ends his poem with David's speech, leaving behind the implication that the *moral* action of the story, at any rate, has been resolved by the king's triumphant reassertion of his royal authority. Swift, though he had the chance to extend his work later, preferred to retain his history's original stopping point, and so he too finishes on a triumphant note. Thus, the misnamed *History of the Four Last Years of the Queen* does not carry the narrative up to the queen's death and the consequent ascendancy of the Whigs; instead it ends upon the signing of the Peace of Utrecht—with the queen again "firm" and "steady" and the disrupters of society foiled by her resolution.

Swift was doubtless familiar with his cousin's poem, but in pointing out the above parallels I do not mean to suggest that the two works are closely allied or that Swift necessarily had Dryden's poem in mind as he wrote. The *Four Last Years of the Queen* and *Absalom and Achitophel* display some interesting analogies, but inevitably there are more differences between them than resemblances. The real nature of their kinship lies in historical viewpoint and dramatic situation. Both works are variations on the same fundamental political morality play, wherein an indulgent monarch, at first reluctant to exercise his rightful authority, is challenged by a royal favorite who has become a would-be usurper; there ensues a conspiracy against the throne by those who presume to positions beyond their normal places in the social pyramid; and, finally, proper order is restored by an assertion of power from the throne. In the late seventeenth and early eighteenth centuries, with Cromwell's Commonwealth and Monmouth's rebellion fresh in mind, the basic situation portrayed in these two works was one central to contemporary experience, and it functioned, accordingly, as a sort of archetypal social crisis of the age.

Anne's triumph recorded in the *Four Last Years of the Queen* proved to be short lived, and with the collapse of the Tory ministry in 1714 came the materialization of Swift's fears that "malicious pens" would seek to distort the history of the dead queen's reign. From his Irish exile, Swift urged the deposed ministers to vindicate themselves before posterity by

writing full and honest memoirs of their years in office. Neither man
could afford to be quite so indiscreet, though at first both seem to have led
Swift to believe that they would comply. By 1719, however, it had
become apparent that neither St. John nor Harley (procrastinating, as
ever) was likely to provide the desired history, and so Swift resumed his
earlier intention to write one himself. In May, 1719, he writes St. John:
". . . despairing ever to see any thing of what you tell me, [I] have been
some time providing materials for such a work, only upon the strength of
having been always amongst you, and used with more kindness and
confidence, that [*sic*] it often happens to men of my trade and level"
(*Correspondence*, II, 321).

Four years later, Swift was still planning his history, and in a letter of
November 6, 1723, he banteringly assures Harley that "It is destined that
you should have great obligations to me, for who else knows how to
deliver you down to posterity . . ." (*Correspondence*, II, 468). At Harley's death a few months later, Swift's plans became more pressing, and
on July 9, 1724, he solicited Harley's son for permission to inspect those
of the late minister's papers that would be relevant to a history of his
administration: "I have formerly gathered severall Hints, but want many
Materialls . . . which might be easily supplyed. And such a Work most
properly belongs to me, who loved and respected him above all Men, and
had the Honor to know him better than any other of my Level did"
(*Correspondence*, III, 19). Harley's son, no more inclined than his father
had been to revive debate upon potentially embarrassing subjects, politely
evaded Swift's request, as well as a second query sent on July 18, 1726.
This lack of encouragement, combined after a few years with Swift's
advancing age and illness, finally led to abandonment of the project.

Since Swift never got his desired chance to write the "real" *History of
the Four Last Years of the Queen,* we can only speculate as to what form
such a work might have taken. Despite his promises of an "impartial"
account, it seems unlikely that Swift's projected history would have
differed much in partisan fervor from his Tory tracts. The evidence of
Swift's later career scarcely suggests that the passage of time had softened
his fierce animosity toward the Whigs: the battle which had been so
gloriously fought against them might be over, but for Swift the war
against what they represented was waging no less furiously than ever.
Swift's major concession to historical detachment, we may assume, would

have been a greater willingness to offer criticism of Tory tactics and leadership, as he does to some extent in the analytical tracts he composed after the downfall of the Harley–St. John ministry. With greater documentation to strengthen its contentions and with hindsight to confirm its apprehensions, Swift's projected full-scale version of the national crisis in which he had been so aroused a participant would surely have been a more imposing work than the largely occasional writings of 1710–14 that were to have been its preliminary sketches. However, there is no reason to believe that an increase in scope and formality would have resulted in any material change in Swift's earlier conception of the dramatic nature of the story he had to tell and of the fundamental lessons society might derive from it.

Eight: The Uses of *Saeva Indignatio*

I<small>T</small> was with a deep sense of gloom and defeat that Swift
resigned himself to his retirement in Ireland after the downfall of the
Harley–St. John ministry. As he wrote to Vanessa: "At my first coming
I thought I should have dyed with Discontent, and was horribly melancholy while they were installing me [as Dean of St. Patrick's], but it
begins to wear off, and change to Dullness."[1] Behind him in England
the Tories were crushed politically and even in some danger physically—
within a year of the Whig ascendancy, charges of treason in office had
led to Harley's imprisonment and St. John's flight to the Continent. To
the triumphant Whigs of Ireland, Swift himself was no less suspect,
and it seemed prudent for the time being to withdraw into a life of
seclusion wherein his major concerns, as he explained them in a letter
to Alexander Pope on June 28, 1715, became "defending my small
dominions against the Arch-Bishop, and endeavouring to reduce my
rebellious Choir" (Correspondence, II, 177). The mood expressed in
this letter was to last for six years, and from 1714 to 1720 Swift would
write almost nothing except a few semiprivate memoirs and verses.
Before this long public silence came to a close, Swift had had ample
time and occasion to reflect upon the events that had preceded his
exile and to digest the lessons which his years as a Tory rhetorician had
taught him.

In the undated fragments called *Of Publick Absurdityes in England,*
Swift wrote that any man, after viewing the evils and follies of society,
would "with great reason be tempted, according to the present turn of his
humor, either to laugh, lament, or be angry, or if he were sanguin
enough, perhaps to dream of a remedy."[2] The experience of 1710–14 had
taught Swift that laughter, lamentation, and anger, however satisfying,

were in themselves largely ineffective unless they were widespread and coupled with a call to action. Accordingly, he had begun "to dream of a remedy," and when at last he emerged from his political retirement to publish the first of his Irish tracts, *A Proposal for the Universal Use of Irish Manufacture* (1720), he offered his readers a work which was, as Herbert Davis has said, "no mere literary production—it was political satire and political action." [3]

In rousing the people of Ireland to resist English encroachments upon Irish liberties, Swift was fighting a new battle in the continuing war with his old Whig enemies and all they stood for in his mind. The tyranny of the English in Ireland was only another aspect of the same forces which had produced the corruptions in letters and religion that Swift had attacked as early as the *Tale of a Tub.* Swift is no longer content, however, merely to register his amusement or irritation over the spectacle. The advantages of a focused objective had been impressed upon Swift by his experience as a Tory pamphleteer, and it is significant that in nearly all his Irish tracts Swift urges specific action—a boycott, new legislation, or (more characteristically) a repeal of recent innovations and a return to older and sounder policy. The lesson is spelled out in the *Letter to a Young Clergyman* (written in 1719–20—just prior to his first Irish tracts), where he commends Demosthenes and Cicero as models of eloquence, pointing out that "the constant Design of both . . . in all their Speeches, was to drive some one particular Point; either the Condemnation, or Acquittal of an accused Person; a persuasive to War, the enforcing of a Law, and the like" (*Prose Works,* IX, 69). It is likewise noteworthy that in his Irish tracts Swift does not often address himself, as he had so frequently in his pre-1710 productions, to a limited circle of wits and political sophisticates. These might best appreciate his nuances and satirical skill, but it was *popular* opinion that Swift now wished to manipulate. Thus he directs his campaign toward the Irish middle class, particularly the shopkeepers, who, unlike their richer, more politically self-conscious equivalents in England, had not developed into a "Monied-Interest" threatening the traditional order.

The problems of addressing himself to an audience which on its lower fringes was only semiliterate were not altogether new to Swift. Although he had scorned such readers while in London and had affected to despise writers, like Defoe, who catered to "the lowest Understanding," his own experience as a preacher had given him much valuable training in adapting his style and arguments to the requirements of an audience with limited or nonexistent formal education. Swift's advice about preaching and prose style, as recorded in a *Letter to a Young Clergyman* and elsewhere, emphasizes the necessity of simplicity and clarity. It is of primary importance, he explains to the young clergyman, that the language used in a sermon be easily understood and free of either obscure vocabulary, esoteric reference, or confusing verbal embellishments; "For a Divine hath nothing to say to the wisest Congregation of any Parish in this Kingdom, which he may not express in a Manner to be understood by the meanest among them" (*Prose Works*, IX, 66).

In his own sermons Swift quite literally practices what he preaches, and, in accordance with his awareness of the average congregation's educational level, he not only strives above all for clarity, but more often than not he includes an explicit promise that he will do so. Thus, in his sermon *On the Poor Man's Contentment,* he remarks: "Now, since a great Part of those, who usually make up our Congregations, are not of considerable Station, and many among them of the lower Sort . . . I thought it might be useful to reason upon this Point in as plain a Manner as I can" (*Prose Works,* IX, 190–91). Likewise, in *On the Testimony of Conscience* he announces: "I shall explain it [i.e., conscience] to you in the clearest manner I am able" (*Prose Works,* IX, 150). And again, in his sermon *On the Trinity,* he tells his hearers: ". . . I hope, to handle [the subject] in such a Manner, that the most Ignorant among you may return home better informed of your Duty in this great Point, than probably you are at present" (*Prose Works,* IX, 159). Swift is as good as his promise, and his sermons are models of lucid, if somewhat patronizing, presentation.*

The audience toward which Swift directed his Irish tracts was essentially only a larger version of his congregation at St. Patrick's. Although

* The majority of Swift's congregation would probably have been pleased, rather than offended, by the note of condescension in his sermons. Many preachers of the day, as Swift's comments imply, confused their listeners with flowery or abstruse orations designed for self-display and publication. Swift's congregation could, at any rate, be sure that his sermons had been written with no outside audience in mind. Swift himself seems to have considered his sermons as purely occasional. He made no effort to preserve them, and the few that have survived have done so by chance.

the members of Swift's parish, as Church of Ireland communicants and as city dwellers, were part of a national minority, in terms of their economic and educational range, they furnished a reasonably accurate cross-section of the literate populace. Hitherto, it was only in his sermons that Swift had found occasion to address so inclusive an audience, and we have seen how the very idea of writing for the "vulgar Sort" had earlier won his scorn. By 1720, however, the political consciousness and polemical purpose which Swift had developed during his years as a Tory pamphleteer led him to recognize the importance of focusing his works upon practical persuasive goals. In the case of the Irish tracts, these goals required widespread action, and accordingly, Swift conscientiously bent his efforts toward reaching the broadest possible mass of readers.

Swift's approach in the *Drapier's Letters* clearly demonstrates his skillful gauging of his audience and its needs. The first of the *Drapier's Letters* is characterized on its title page as "Very Proper to be kept in every FAMILY," and is formally addressed to "the *Shop-Keepers, Tradesmen, Farmers,* and *Common-People* of IRELAND" (*Prose Works,* X, 1). This is Swift's basic audience, though he does not totally ignore other classes. One whole letter (number 3, *Some Observations upon a Report of the Committee Relating to Wood's Half-Pence*) is devoted ostensibly at least *"To the Nobility and Gentry of the Kingdom of* IRELAND" (*Prose Works,* X, 27), and the fourth letter (addressed "to the whole People of IRELAND") is more specifically directed to the Anglo-Irish Protestant minority.[4] But although the Protestant ruling classes entered into Swift's scheme, they formed only a tiny portion of those whose help was needed to achieve his specific goal—the organization of an effective boycott of Wood's coinage. For this purpose, it was necessary to elicit the cooperation of Ireland's aforementioned *"Shop-Keepers, Tradesmen, Farmers, and Common-People"* (in precisely that order of importance), and so with these readers in mind Swift designed his persona, his language, and his major appeals.

In the remarks Swift makes by way of introduction to his first *Drapier's Letter* there is a clear echo of the tone he habitually employed toward the equivalent audience in his sermons:

What I intend now to say to you, is . . . of the greatest Concern to your selves. . . . Therefore I do most earnestly exhort you as *Men,* as *Christians,* as

Parents, and as *Lovers of your Country,* to read this Paper with the utmost Attention, or get it read to you by others; which that you may do at the less Expence, I have ordered the Printer to sell it at the lowest Rate. [*Prose Works,* X, 3]

The stance of the preacher addressing his flock becomes stronger still in his announcement a little later: "I will . . . first tell you the *plain Story of the Fact;* and then I will lay before you, how you ought to act in common Prudence, and according to the *Laws of your Country.*" But though the Drapier may occasionally assume a lofty pulpit manner, he is more often at pains to assure his readers that he is a plain and ordinary man, without pretense to great knowledge or education. Thus, when he discusses the legality of Wood's patent, he explains that he is merely repeating "the Judgments of some great *Lawyers* . . . whom I fee'd [*sic*] on purpose for your Sakes. . . ." Likewise, after quoting a Parliamentary report in Wood's favor, he despairingly asks (preparatory to a demolishing reply): "How shall I, a poor ignorant Shop-keeper, utterly unskilled in Law, be able to answer so weighty an Objection?" (*Prose Works,* X, 4, 8–9, 29).

However humble he may be (or pretend to be) in approaching points of law, the Drapier is bold and authoritative in discussing the practical realities of the marketplace. He derives his self-confidence from his commercial success, for Swift, in order to emphasize the disinterested patriotism of the Drapier's motives, has made him a man of some substance. Though in his first letter the Drapier modestly describes himself as having "a pretty good Shop of *Irish Stuffs* and *Silks,*" by his second letter he complacently remarks, "I am no inconsiderable Shop-keeper in this Town," and later he explains: "I have no Interest in this Affair, but what is common to the Publick: I can live better than many others: I have some Gold and Silver by me, and a Shop well furnished; and shall be able to make a Shift, when many of my Betters are starving." As a prosperous, though petty, tradesman, Swift's Drapier is in the advantageous position of being both humble enough to elicit a sense of self-identification from his lower- and middle-class readers, and at the same time imposing enough to give appropriate force to his sneers at Wood as a *"Hard-ware-Man,"* a "diminutive, insignificant Mechanick," and an "obscure *Ironmonger*" (*Prose Works,* X, 7, 16, 19, 22, 54). The Drapier's audience, which itself included many who were socially and eco-

nomically "diminutive," "insignificant," and "obscure," might have
resented such epithets had they come from a lord, but when the dis-
paragement came, as it were, from a member of the family (and when
the object was a hated foreign enemy), even the lowliest of readers was
likely to be in sympathy with the sentiment.

In keeping with the Drapier's character and his audience's requirements, Swift writes in a style that is deliberately undistinguished. The
Drapier has no hesitation in using the sort of platitudes ("a Word to the
Wise is enough") that a purist like Swift normally avoids. Nearly all the
Drapier's literary allusions, as might be expected from a man who is
largely self-educated, are from the Bible. On one occasion, when he
employs the abbreviation, "N.B.," he feels obliged to explain this esoteric
usage with a parenthetical "(that is to say *Nota Bene,* or *Mark Well*)."
The Drapier's only stylistic flourishes are his metaphors, most of which
are drawn from the world of petty commerce. Likewise, it is the viewpoint
of the small tradesman which is foremost in the examples that are used to
illustrate the havoc Wood's debased coinage might spread. Thus, in one
place the Drapier predicts that acceptance of Wood's "Trash" might
mean that a squire buying clothes would need to bring along a whole
cartload of coins. It is characteristic of the Drapier that in making this
point, he solicits his readers' fullest sympathies *not* for the squire who
would be obliged to carry so many coins, but for the harried shopkeeper
who might be forced to accept them in payment.

In the Drapier, Swift, for the first time in a major work, offers his
readers a fully conceived fictional persona with whom they are seriously
invited to identify themselves. Figures like Isaac Bickerstaff and the
narrator of the *Tale of a Tub* were intended above all as objects of
ridicule, and to accept them at face value would be to miss Swift's whole
satiric message. The Drapier, however, is designed to achieve rapport with
the audience, not to inspire its laughter. His style is neither parodied nor
burlesqued, as is usually the case with Swift's earlier personae; instead, it
is a sort of pastiche of the style one might expect from such a man. The
knowing, who quickly detected Swift's authorship of the *Drapier's Letters,*
could smile at the irony implicit in such a mask, but the Drapier himself
(despite a few sly touches) is not conceived of as an essentially comic
figure. He is the author's mouthpiece, used in much the same way that
Defoe uses Robinson Crusoe—to represent his creator's own point of

view, articulated in the manner best suited for the persuasion of his intended audience. The degree of precision with which Swift calculated the Drapier's audience and its requirements can be gauged by the tangible results his tracts produced.[5] The Drapier's call to action was answered almost at once. When it arrived in Ireland, Wood's coinage was greeted by an effective popular boycott, and it was not until 1737, when Walpole lowered the gold standard and refused Ireland the right to coin her own money, that English coinage was finally imposed upon the Irish. In terms of immediate and measurable (if impermanent) impact, therefore, the *Drapier's Letters* stand second only to *Conduct of the Allies* as Swift's most successful efforts in political persuasion.*

Since the Irish tracts most clearly display Swift's post-1714 sense of urgency and his resultant focus upon audience and polemical purpose, I have used the *Drapier's Letters* to illustrate the nature of the impetus Swift derived from his experience as a Tory pamphleteer. Unlike his more purely political writings, Swift's complex masterpiece, *Gulliver's Travels,* is ultimately a unique work of art, and, as such, does not lend itself to classification or inclusion in any simple pattern. Nevertheless, *Gulliver's Travels* is, among other things, a polemical tract par excellence, and its survival today—not merely as a library piece, but as a living work read by millions—is a tribute to Swift's success in designing his work to meet the varied needs of an avowed audience of awesome inclusiveness. For it was Swift's ambitious intention that *Gulliver's Travels* should reach every layer of the social hierarchy, and his audience, accordingly, is nothing less than mankind itself. To a far greater degree than most books so addressed, *Gulliver* may be said to have won the attention of its audience, though this success has not always been attended by results of the sort Swift hoped for.

It has frequently been remarked that Swift himself could scarcely have conceived of a circumstance more pointedly ironic than that this, the bitterest of his satires, should have become a popular children's classic, having suffered only minor expurgations in the process. In a very real sense, however, such a fate was included in Swift's plans for the work, for *Gulliver's Travels* is so constructed as to have meaning on one level or

* I am speaking here with reference only to practical results. In terms of artistic force and effect, the *Modest Proposal,* of course, is infinitely superior to both works I have cited.

another for almost any conceivable reader. If *Gulliver's Travels* has
flourished in the nursery, it has also become the object of so much
scholarly interpretation and commentary that one is often uncomfortably
reminded of Gulliver's own remarks concerning the embarrassing contrast between Aristotle and the vast tribe of his explicators. Ten days after
the publication of the book, John Gay wrote Swift (November 17,
1726): "From the highest to the lowest it is universally read, from the
Cabinet-council to the Nursery. . . . It hath pass'd Lords and Commons,
nemine contradicente; and the whole town, men, women, and children
are quite full of it" (*Correspondence,* III, 182–83). The subsequent
history of *Gulliver's Travels* would seem to indicate that Gay was not
exaggerating the range of audience from which the work elicited a strong
and immediate response. The very young and the very naïve could read it
as a fabulous adventure story; the moderately perceptive could in addition
detect its parable of human vanity; and the sophisticated could add to
their enjoyment of the story's simpler levels by savoring all or part of its
intricate personal and political allegories. Swift's intention embraces all of
these readings, for he has created in Gulliver a persona who serves as all
things to all men. Thus, to the knowing reader, Gulliver, like the "author" of the *Tale of a Tub,* appears a colossal fool, but since he sometimes
functions, like the Drapier, as Swift's spokesman, the story can be read at
one stage of awareness as a glorification of its narrator.

On October 15, 1725, Pope wrote chidingly to Swift:

I have often imagined to myself, that if ever All of us [i.e., Harley, St. John,
Swift, Arbuthnot] met again, after so many Varieties and Changes . . . that
we shou'd meet like the Righteous in the Millennium, quite in peace,
divested of all our former passions. . . . But I find you would rather be
employ'd as an Avenging Angel of wrath, to break your Vial of Indignation
over the heads of the wretched, pitiful creatures of this World; nay would
make them *Eat your Book* [*Gulliver's Travels*], which you have made as
bitter a pill for them as possible. [*Correspondence,* III, 107–8]

Swift's reply was emphatic: "Drown the World, I am not content with
despising it, but I would anger it if I could with safety" (*Correspondence,*
III, 117). The man who wrote *Gulliver's Travels* in order to "anger" the
world had come a long way from the young author who twenty-five years
earlier had been content to despise it. Something of the change can be
traced in Swift's varying treatments of a similar theme in the *Tale of a*

Tub, the *Conduct of the Allies,* and *Gulliver's Travels.* In the *Tale of a Tub* the young Swift had speculated over the reasons that inspire princes to wage war, and after a great show of mock-solemnity he had announced that noxious bodily spirits were the motivating factors. With a wealth of allusion to Lucretius, Paracelsus, and an unnamed "very antient Author," he had explained how frustrated love and similar irritants often created dangerous vapors in the lower parts of the body, and how such vapors, if unchecked, could ascend to the brain and inspire bellicosity and dreams of military glory. Accordingly, he had arrived at the inescapable conclusion (two hundred years before Freud) that

The very same Principle that influences a *Bully* to break the Windows of a Whore, who has jilted him, naturally stirs up a Great Prince to raise mighty Armies, and dream of nothing but Sieges, Battles, and Victories. . . . The same Spirits which in their superior Progress would conquer a Kingdom, descending upon the *Anus,* conclude in a *Fistula.* [*Prose Works,* I, 104]

Seven years after the *Tale of a Tub,* Swift turned again to the "Motives that may engage a wise Prince or State in a War," but this time without satire, esoteric allusion, or frivolity. The *Conduct of the Allies* was designed to convince rural squires, not to amuse coffee-house wits, and Swift's tone had changed to one of sober discussion, as he pointed out (prior to urging an end to the War of the Spanish Succession) that a prince or nation might justly resort to arms in order to check "the overgrown Power of some ambitious Neighbour; to recover what hath been unjustly taken from Them; to revenge some Injury They have received; . . . to assist some Ally in a just Quarrel; or lastly, to defend Themselves when They are invaded" (*Prose Works,* VI, 7).

It was not until *Gulliver's Travels,* however, that Swift issued his final opinions upon this subject. Twenty-two years after the *Tale of a Tub* and fifteen years after *Conduct of the Allies,* Swift addressed himself once more to the task of explaining "the Causes or Motives that made one Country go to War with another." This time the reasons, as Gulliver outlines them to his Houyhnhnm master, have become uniformly ignoble.

It is a very justifiable Cause of War to invade a Country after the People have been wasted by Famine. . . . It is justifiable to enter into a War against our nearest Ally, when one of his Towns lies convenient for us. . . . If a Prince send Forces into a Nation, where the People are poor and ignorant, he may

lawfully put half of them to Death, and make Slaves of the rest. . . . It is a
very kingly, honourable, and frequent Practice, when one Prince desires the
Assistance of another . . . that the Assistant . . . should seize on the Dominions himself, and kill, imprison or banish the Prince he came to relieve.
[*Prose Works*, XI, 246]

Gulliver's list differs from the others in that it is not primarily designed to
elicit either the reader's laughter or his mere intellectual agreement—it is
meant to shock and appall him into sharing Swift's own disquieting
awareness of "the Treasure of Baseness in Man." * In the bitter progression Swift was to make from the amused banter of the *Tale of a Tub* to
the despairing gloom of *Gulliver's Travels,* the aroused moral earnestness
of the *Conduct of the Allies* and the rest of the Tory tracts marks a
significant transition toward the ultimate *saeva indignatio* which impelled
Swift to vex the world instead of diverting it.

The majority of this study has been devoted to a discussion of the
specific persuasive techniques Swift employed in his Tory tracts, and it
would not be difficult to point out general parallels of practice and
approach between his Tory tracts and his more famous later works. But to
do so would not be to demonstrate any meaningful technical "influence."
Swift does not seem to have been one of those writers who gradually
develop increasing skills through the course of a long career. His earliest
prose work, the *Tale of a Tub,* is in many ways the most technically
accomplished performance of his whole career. Swift doubtless profited
from his 1710–14 training in the use of rhetorical devices, but the real
influence of these years lay elsewhere, and I have tried here to suggest its
nature.

"There are two Ends that Men propose in writing Satyr," Swift wrote
in 1728, "one of them less noble than the other, as regarding nothing
further than the private Satisfaction, and Pleasure of the Writer; but
without any View towards *personal Malice:* The other is a *publick Spirit,*
prompting Men of *Genius* and Virtue, to mend the World as far as they
are able" (*Prose Works*, XII, 34). It has been my contention that prior

---

* It is worth noting that Thursday, September 7, 1710—the day Gulliver
set sail from Portsmouth on the voyage that was to carry him to Houyhnhnm-
land and misanthropy—was the same day that his creator had arrived in
London for what developed into a four year stay and his new career as a Tory
pamphleteer.

to 1710 Swift's writings were largely of the first sort, and that his experience as a Tory pamphleteer gave rise to a sense of urgency which led him thereafter to aim for the more "noble" end of trying "to mend the World." As the Tory debacle of 1714 approached, Swift wrote to Arbuthnot: ". . . I am angry at those who disperse us sooner than there was need. I have a Mind to be very angry, and to let my anger break out in some manner that will not please them, at the End of a Pen" (*Correspondence,* II, 36). The rest of Swift's career was devoted to carrying out that impulse, not merely against the Whigs, but against all the forces of fanaticism, corruption, and oppression they represented in his mind. The world's small legacy of immortal literary works has been immeasurably enriched by his anger.

Notes

INTRODUCTION

1. Jonathan Swift, *Journal to Stella,* ed. Sir Harold Williams (Oxford, 1948), I, 24.

2. *The Poems of Jonathan Swift,* ed. Sir Harold Williams (Oxford, 1957), I, 96.

3. *The Correspondence of Jonathan Swift,* ed. Sir Harold Williams (Oxford, 1963–65), I, 166.

4. For an account of Swift's literary and political relationship with Addison and Steele, see Bertrand A. Goldgar, *The Curse of Party: Swift's Relations with Addison and Steele* (Lincoln, Neb., 1961).

5. For a detailed consideration of the Whig and Tory elements in Swift's pre-1710 writings, see Robert W. Babcock, "Swift's Conversion to the Tory Party," *University of Michigan Publications in Language and Literature* (*Essays and Studies in English and Comparative Literature*), VIII (1932), 133–49.

6. *The Prose Works of Jonathan Swift,* ed. Herbert Davis (Oxford, 1937————), VII, xxxiv–xxxv.

7. Bernard Acworth, *Swift* (London, 1947), p. 145.

8. John, Earl of Orrery, *Remarks on the Life and Writings of Dr. Jonathan Swift* (London, 1752), pp. 29–30.

9. See *Prose Works,* VII, Appendix C, 181–218.

10. For a brief, documented account of Harley and St. John's exchanges with the Pretender, see G. M. Trevelyan's *England Under Queen Anne* (London, 1948), III, 336–40. Of this correspondence, Trevelyan remarks:

[The] English Ministers wrote nothing direct to the Prentender, but they sent him continual messages and promises and received his answers through the agency of Gaultier and Torcy. The degree of their sincerity, especially in the case of Oxford, is open to endless question, but the facts of this intrigue are to be found in the French Foreign Office Archives (*Affaires étrangères, Angleterre*), in the Quai d'Orsay.

CHAPTER ONE

1. *The Prose Works of Jonathan Swift,* ed. Herbert Davis (Oxford, 1937————), I, 1. All parenthetical references within the text are to volume and page in this edition, unless otherwise identified.

2. *The Correspondence of Jonathan Swift,* ed. Sir Harold Williams (Oxford, 1963–65), III, 102.

3. Samuel Johnson, *Lives of the English Poets,* ed. G. B. Hill (Oxford, 1905), III, 51.

4. See Irvin Ehrenpreis, *Swift: The Man, His Works, and the Age* (Cambridge, Mass., 1962), I, 186–87.

5. As quoted in the introduction to Swift's *Tale of a Tub,* ed. A. C. Guthkelch and D. Nichol Smith (Oxford, 1957), p. xlviii.

6. Ricardo Quintana, *Swift: An Introduction* (London, 1955), p. 81.

7. John, Earl of Orrery, *Remarks on the Life and Writings of Dr. Jonathan Swift* (London, 1752), p. 62.

8. As quoted by R. L. Brett, *The Third Earl of Shaftesbury: A Study in Eighteenth-Century Literary Theory* (London, 1951), pp. 167–68.

9. For a discussion of the early eighteenth-century distrust of wit as a danger to religion, see Edward Niles Hooker, "Pope on Wit: *The Essay on Criticism,*" *Eighteenth-Century English Literature: Modern Essays in Criticism,* ed. James L. Clifford (New York, 1959), pp. 42–61.

10. For a further discussion of Swift's theories of history, see James W. Johnson, "Scythia, Cato, and Corruption: Swift's Historical Concepts and Their Background" (Ph.D. dissertation, Vanderbilt University, 1954); Louis Bredvold, "The Gloom of the Tory Satirists," *Eighteenth-Century English Literature: Modern Essays in Criticism,* ed. James L. Clifford (New York, 1959), pp. 3–20; and Irvin Ehrenpreis, *The Personality of Jonathan Swift* (London, 1958), pp. 59–82.

11. Herbert Davis, *The Satire of Jonathan Swift* (New York, 1947), p. 7.

CHAPTER TWO

1. *Rhetoric of Aristotle,* trans. Lane Cooper (New York, 1932), I, 1–7.

2. *The Prose Works of Jonathan Swift,* ed. Herbert Davis (Oxford, 1937————), VI, 71. All parenthetical references within the text are to volume and page of this edition.

3. Robert Walcott, *English Politics in the Early Eighteenth Century* (Cambridge, Mass., 1956), pp. 9–10.

4. Sir Lewis Namier, *The Structure of Politics at the Accession of George III* (London, 1957), p. 68.

5. Dorothy Marshall, *English People in the Eighteenth Century* (London, 1956), p. 42.

6. J. H. Plumb, *England in the Eighteenth Century* (London, 1955), p. 19.

7. Jonathan Swift, *Journal to Stella,* ed. Sir Harold Williams (Oxford, 1948), II, 441.

8. As quoted by Herbert Davis in his introduction to Swift's *Prose Works,* VI, xv.

9. *The Manuscripts of His Grace the Duke of Portland, Preserved at Welbeck Abbey,* Historical Manuscripts Commission (London, 1897), IV, 641.

10. *Ibid.,* VII, 79.

CHAPTER THREE

1. See Wilbur S. Howell, *Logic and Rhetoric in England, 1500–1700* (Princeton, N. J., 1956); and Donald L. Clark, *John Milton at St. Paul's School* (New York, 1948).

2. For information on Swift's study of rhetoric, see Charles A. Beaumont, *Swift's Classical Rhetoric* (Athens, Ga., 1961), pp. 1–14; and Irvin Ehrenpreis, *Swift: The Man, His Works, and the Age* (Cambridge, Mass., 1962), I, 38, 59, 199–200.

3. *The Prose Works of Jonathan Swift,* ed. Herbert Davis (Oxford, 1937————), V, 345. All parenthetical references within the text are to volume and page of this edition.

4. *Ibid.,* XI, 197. For a discussion of Swift's attitude toward Aristotle and his rhetorical doctrines see John M. Bullitt, *Jonathan Swift and the Anatomy of Satire* (Cambridge, Mass., 1953), pp. 68–75.

5. William Ewald, *The Masks of Jonathan Swift* (Cambridge, Mass., 1954), p. 74.

6. See Chapter Four, note 5.

7. Edward W. Rosenheim, Jr., in his *Swift and the Satirist's Art* (Chicago, 1963), pp. 12–14, distinguishes between "punitive" satire (in which the satirist attacks an object which both he and his audience assume a priori to be deserving of such attack) and "persuasive" satire (in which the satirist seeks to *convince* his audience that the object under attack deserves opprobrium). Swift's satire in his briefer Tory tracts falls into both categories. On most occasions, knowing that his audience is predisposed toward the Tory cause, Swift's satire (and indeed his nonsatiric rhetoric) is primarily punitive. In

those cases where he is less certain of his audience's sympathies (e.g., his initial attacks upon Marlborough), his satire becomes persuasive in emphasis.

8. John Locke, *Essay Concerning Human Understanding,* III, 10, 34.

9. See John R. Moore, "Was Jonathan Swift a Moderate?" *South Atlantic Quarterly,* LIII, No. 2 (1954), 260–67.

10. Samuel Johnson, *Lives of the English Poets,* ed. G. B. Hill (Oxford, 1905), III, 19.

CHAPTER FOUR

1. *The Prose Works of Jonathan Swift,* ed. Herbert Davis (Oxford, 1937———), VIII, 14–15. All parenthetical references within the text are to volume and page of this edition.

2. In the last fifteen years Swift's use of rhetorical techniques, primarily in his satirical works, has been the subject of considerable study. See John M. Bullitt, *Jonathan Swift and the Anatomy of Satire* (Cambridge, Mass., 1953); Martin Price, *Swift's Rhetorical Art* (New Haven, Conn., 1953); and Charles A. Beaumont, *Swift's Classical Rhetoric* (Athens, Ga., 1961).

3. See Bullitt, *Anatomy of Satire,* pp. 88–92, for a discussion of Swift's argument by means of analogy, particularly in the *Drapier's Letters.*

4. Samuel Johnson, *Lives of the English Poets,* ed. G. B. Hill (Oxford, 1905), III, 51.

5. On April 8, 1738, Erasmus Lewis, in response to Swift's renewed plans to publish the *Four Last Years of the Queen,* wrote Swift, saying that certain objections had been made to the manuscript by "Lord O[xfor]d [Harley's son], and two or three more . . . zealous for your fame and safety. . . ." These objections Lewis gives as follows:

1*st,* They conceive the first establishment of the South Sea Company is not rightly stated. . . .
2*d,* They think the transactions with Mr. Buys might have been represented in a more advantageous light, and more to the honour of that administration, and, undoubtedly they would have been so by your pen, had you been master of all the facts.
3*d,* The D[uke] of M[arlborough]'s courage not to be called in question.
4*th,* The projected design of an assassination [of Harley] they believe true, but that a matter of so high a nature ought not to be asserted without exhibiting the proofs.
5*th,* The present Ministers, who are the rump of those whose characters you have painted, shew too plainly, that they have not acted upon republican, or, indeed, any other principles than those of interest and ambition.
6*th,* Now, I have mentioned characters, I must tell you that they were clearly

of opinion, that if those you have drawn should be published as they now stand, nothing could save the author's printer and publishers from some grievous punishment.

The letter has been endorsed in Swift's hand: "On some mistakes in the History of Four Last Years. *Mon ami prudent*" (*The Correspondence of Jonathan Swift,* ed. Sir Harold Williams [Oxford, 1963–65], V, 104–6).

CHAPTER FIVE

1. *The Prose Works of Jonathan Swift,* ed. Herbert Davis (Oxford, 1937————), IV, 243. All parenthetical references within the text are to volume and page of this edition.

2. For the development of the Character tradition, see Benjamin Boyce, *The Theophrastan Character in England to 1642* (Cambridge, Mass., 1947) and *The Polemic Character: 1640–1661* (Lincoln, Neb., 1955); and D. Nichol Smith, *Characters from the Histories & Memoirs of the Seventeenth Century* (Oxford, 1920).

3. *The Correspondence of Jonathan Swift,* ed. Sir Harold Williams (Oxford, 1963–65), III, 118.

4. In his *Proposal for Correcting, Improving and Ascertaining the English Tongue* (1712) Swift appears as a projector rather than a historian, and accordingly he feels free to praise Harley (to whom the tract is addressed) by means of raillery.

I know not whether that which I am going to say, may pass for Caution, Advice, or Reproach; any of which will be justly thought very improper from one in my Station, to one in yours. However, I must venture to affirm that if Genius and Learning be not encouraged under your Lordship's Administration, you are the most inexcusable Person alive. . . . I know, my Lord, your Friends will offer in your Defence, that in your private Capacity, you never refused your Purse and Credit to the Service and Support of learned or ingenious Men: And that ever since you have been in publick Employment, you have constantly bestowed your Favours to the most deserving Persons. But I desire your Lordship not to be deceived: We never will admit of these Excuses; nor will allow your private Liberality, as great as it is, to attone for your excessive publick Thrift. But here again, I am afraid most good Subjects will interpose in your Defence, by alledging [*sic*] the desperate Condition you found the Nation in, and the Necessity there was for . . . the utmost Frugality. We grant all this, my Lord; but then, it ought likewise to be considered, that you have already saved several Millions to the Publick; and that what we ask is too inconsiderable to break into any Rules of the strictest good Husbandry. [*Prose Works,* IV, 19–20]

CHAPTER SIX

1. Daniel Defoe, *The Review* (Facsimile Text Society; New York, 1938).

2. John F. Ross, *Swift and Defoe: A Study in Relationship* (University of California Publications in English, Vol. II; Berkeley, 1941).

3. *The Prose Works of Jonathan Swift,* ed. Herbert Davis (Oxford, 1937————), II, 113.

4. See Bertrand A. Goldgar, *The Curse of Party: Swift's Relations with Addison and Steele* (Lincoln, Neb., 1961), pp. 126–31.

5. *Review,* I, ii. The volume and page numbers referred to are those of the original.

6. As quoted in Marjorie Nicolson's introduction to *The Best of Defoe's Review,* ed. William L. Payne (New York, 1951), p. xvii, note.

7. As quoted by James Sutherland, *Defoe* (London, 1950), p. 114, note.

8. *Review* (Index), p. 44.

9. *Prose Works,* II, 173; *Tatler* 230, Sept. 28, 1710.

CHAPTER SEVEN

1. John, Earl of Orrery, *Remarks on the Life and Writings of Dr. Jonathan Swift* (London, 1752), pp. 206–7.

2. *The Correspondence of Jonathan Swift,* ed. Sir Harold Williams (Oxford, 1963–65), V, 74.

3. See *The Prose Works of Jonathan Swift,* ed. Herbert Davis (Oxford, 1937————), V, ix–x.

4. *Letters of Jonathan Swift to Charles Ford,* ed. D. Nichol Smith (Oxford, 1935), pp. xxxi–xxxii.

5. *The Letters of the Earl of Chesterfield,* ed. John Bradshaw (London, 1926), III, 1217.

6. See Irvin Ehrenpreis, *The Personality of Jonathan Swift* (London, 1958), pp. 75–80.

7. *Ibid.,* p. 64.

8. *The Works of Sir William Temple* (London, 1770), III, 44–45.

9. *Prose Works,* XI, 124. Swift's ideas on society and social order are illuminatingly discussed in Kathleen Williams' *Jonathan Swift and the Age of Compromise* (Lawrence, Kan., 1958), pp. 91–117.

10. See Jonathan Swift, *Journal to Stella,* ed. Sir Harold Williams (Oxford, 1948), I, 263–64.

11. Bernard S. Schilling, *Dryden and the Conservative Myth: A Reading of Absalom and Achitophel* (New Haven, Conn., 1961).

12. All *Absalom and Achitophel* references are taken from *The Poems of John Dryden,* ed. James Kinsley (Oxford, 1958), I, 215–43.

13. *Prose Works,* VII, 125. The restraining orders, which in effect produced a cease-fire during negotiations, were in reality the work of St. John—the queen contributing little more than her signature. In Swift's account, however, the queen for obvious reasons is pictured as the actual rather than the merely symbolic originator of policy.

CHAPTER EIGHT

1. *The Correspondence of Jonathan Swift,* ed. Sir Harold Williams (Oxford, 1963–65), I, 373.

2. *The Prose Works of Jonathan Swift,* ed. Herbert Davis (Oxford, 1937———), V, 79.

3. Herbert Davis, *The Satire of Jonathan Swift* (New York, 1947), p. 66.

4. See Carl Woodring, "The Aims, Audience, and Structure of the Drapier's Fourth Letter," *Modern Language Quarterly,* XVII (1956), 50–59.

5. For an account of the historical background and reception of the *Drapier's Letters,* see Oliver W. Ferguson, *Jonathan Swift and Ireland* (Urbana, Ill., 1962), pp. 83–138.

Index